G000123837

Selling by Telephone

For Alex

THE SUNDAY TIMES

BUSINESS ENTERPRISE GUIDE

Selling by Telephone

How to Turn Business Cold Calling into Hot Profit

4TH EDITION

CHRIS DE WINTER

RECOMMENDED BY
INSTITUTE OF DIRECTORS

KOGAN
PAGE

This book has been endorsed by the Institute of Directors.

The endorsement is given to selected Kogan Page books which the IoD recognises as being of specific interest to its members and providing them with up-to-date, informative and practical resources for creating business success. Kogan Page books endorsed by the IoD represent the most authoritative guidance available on a wide range of subjects including management, finance, marketing, training and HR.

The views expressed in this book are those of the author and are not necessarily the same as those of the Institute of Directors.

First published as *The Secrets of Successful Telephone Selling: How to turn cold calling into hot profit*, 1988 (Hardback), 1989 (Paperback), 1990 (Reprint) by Heinemann Professional Publishing Ltd, Halley Court, Jordan Hill, Oxford OX2 8EJ

Second edition published in 1995 by Kogan Page Ltd
Third edition 1998
Fourth edition 2002

Apart from any fair dealing for the purposes of research or private study, or criticism or review, as permitted under the Copyright, Designs and Patents Act, 1988, this publication may only be reproduced, stored or transmitted, in any form or by any means, with the prior permission in writing of the publishers, or in the case of reprographic reproduction in accordance with the terms of licences issued by the Copyright Licensing Agency. Enquiries concerning reproduction outside those terms should be sent to the publishers at the undermentioned address:

Kogan Page Limited
120 Pentonville Road
London N1 9JN

© Chris de Winter, 1988, 1995, 1998, 2002

The right of Chris de Winter to be identified as the author of this work has been asserted by her in accordance with the Copyright, Designs and Patents Act 1988.

The views expressed in this book are those of the author, and are not necessarily the same as those of Times Newspapers Ltd.

British Library Cataloguing in Publication Data

A CIP record for this book is available from the British Library.

ISBN 0 7494 3682 4

Typeset by Jean Cussons Typesetting, Diss, Norfolk
Printed and bound in Great Britain by Clays Ltd, St Ives plc

Contents

About the author

Chris de Winter received a full grounding in psychology at college where she became a fully trained teacher, before moving into the world of advertising. Her hard-earned experience with Thomson's, one of the UK's acknowledged leaders in sales training, helped to make her a top trainer and manager in her own right.

Since starting her own sales training and management consultancy Chris de Winter has improved sales and communications within numerous companies – from small local firms to large national organisations. The techniques she uses are extremely adaptable to any business environment and size. Once learned and practised they can be applied to any selling situation.

Foreword

This book continues to be a leader in its field. It brings together insight and practical examples in a way that is both persuasive and instructive. The reader can absorb the lessons offered and convert this knowledge into immediate practical achievements when dealing with customers.

In today's world it is increasingly important to be able to communicate effectively with clients as and when it is convenient for them. This has to be balanced by the corporate need to promote products and services offered by your organisation and to provide that extra support to clients which makes successful relationships possible. This book is a clear leader in its field, enabling you to understand the mind of the customer and showing the service provider how to promote products and services without being intrusive.

Technology is providing a number of differing means through which business can be conducted. This technology increasingly provides clearer differentiation and segmentation of the client base, providing complete client histories online and attempting to identify potential client needs.

Within this technological world it is sometimes easy to lose sight of the fact that business is transacted between people – those with needs and expectations and those who can help meet these requirements. If you can harness both the technology and the ability to deal effectively with people then real business opportunities can be opened up.

Communication with the client needs to provide sufficient information to assist with their decision making and should fulfil a professional interest in satisfying the client's needs. It is a company's responsibility to help the client by understanding his or her needs and by narrowing of the field of choice to the products and services that are most suited to them. This requires skill and patience. It requires a teacher's ability to probe and offer, to test and prove, and must conclude with a solution that meets or exceeds the customer's expectations and that has been based on clear and honest exchanges. The solution will then be durable and will result in a profitable long-term relationship with the client.

This book takes you through the process that leads to success and provides clear instructions on how to improve your interaction with the customer. The telephone is a medium of massive potential, much of which is yet to be realised. It allows regular and close contact with the customer and provides timely feedback to ensure that the customer–company relationship remains positive. Talking to people is much more effective than written correspondence: it removes jargon and clever words which can confuse and replaces them with an interactive dialogue that enhances understanding and satisfaction.

In successful business, everyone within a company commits to the idea of service provided utilising traditional values and modern techniques. Trust is established with the client and repeat buying is made possible. This cannot be achieved without the values of the company being evident through the attitude of each member of staff and demonstrated in each transaction. This can be at any time, including during initial contact, when taking orders, following up calls to establish whether the customer has been and continues to be satisfied or simply to keep in touch. This effort inevitably translates into increasingly profitable relationships for all parties.

This book proves it is possible to have your cake and eat it – whether you are a contented customer or a member of a company that gains and retains key business partners. It is full of practical examples, so you can adjust your approach for each customer. It will provide you with the confidence you need when dealing with others. The ability to be successful shines through every page of this book and by the time you reach the final page you just know you can do it too.

Kevin Powell
UK Financial Controller
Royal and Sun Alliance plc

Preface

One of the most astonishing things in business today is that there is still, seemingly, so much controversy surrounding the use of the telephone as a sales tool. Comments such as 'It's so transparent', 'I wouldn't give anyone the time/take the call', 'people prefer face-to-face contact', 'It's just a con' are all too familiar.

The name 'call centre' has helped to defuse the term 'telesales', but many people still feel strongly aggrieved. Yet to dispel any myth regarding the strength of the telephone we have only to glance through the Job Seekers sections of our papers to see evidence that over the last decade telesales vacancies have become increasingly advertised. It isn't just the smaller companies that are advertising either. Large multinationals and corporations have enjoyed rapid expansion in the hands of this very tool. Indeed, many call centres (the generic term for all-embracing teams of telephone operators, from sales to customer service) with sophisticated ACD (Auto Call Distributor) equipment are speeding up the whole telesales operation.

The importance of the telephone in serious business is well recognised. Indeed, 85 per cent of business is now being done by telephone, but many are still learning how best to use it to improve selling effectiveness.

How you view the telephone and the personnel using it is the very key to its success. We live in a world where records and achievements are constantly changing. Just look at the Internet – the speed at which it opens doors is phenomenal. We can't afford to stay still; we have to sharpen our skills and broaden our horizons to stay competitive.

This book has been written and designed to introduce business people to the world of selling over the phone, and how to recruit, train and motivate a telephone selling team. For those already involved and experienced in this form of selling, I hope that it will serve to enhance their existing knowledge and stimulate their thoughts and ideas. In addition, I have added material for professional establishments such as surveyors, engineers and solicitors in the telemarketing section. There has been an increasing demand on them to become more proactive, and this serves to ease the discomfort some may feel.

People who have been in the selling game for a number of years will appreciate that part of the fun of the job is that they are always learning. Nobody can ever be in a position to say, 'I know it all', because the world we live in is subject to constant change. This change affects not only our clients and the markets we serve, but also the products we sell. Since no two calls are the same, we are faced with the constant challenge of keeping ourselves fresh to meet our targets and derive satisfaction from what we are doing. We need to be properly equipped in the latest selling techniques. Once these techniques have been mastered and practised, performance improves, leading to immense job satisfaction and ultimately to a tremendous feeling of success. This is why those of us who set out on a sales career and are bitten by the sales 'bug' usually remain in this field.

As with any other profession, selling needs to be worked at. Yet sheer hard work plays only a small part in the role of salespeople. Success is developed through proper training.

Being able to criticise one's own performance is essential, and the desire to improve can be nurtured by a caring and knowledgeable sales management team. Companies must never forget that while targets need to be reached in the competitive environment we live in, it is our salespeople who present the company's profile to the outside world. It is they who create the vital goodwill of our customers on which business empires depend.

Selling by telephone is undoubtedly one of the major growth areas in the UK at present. It has taken us years to recognise the enormous potential of this form of selling in our business world. Yet telesales people are still being employed and put into place without being properly equipped for the job. Bad scripts, patchy product knowledge and lack of formal training will give a bad impression to our existing and potential clients. The purpose of this book is to demonstrate how correct training and understanding of the problems encountered by telesales personnel can lead to a more fruitful and profitable business.

I have included a comprehensive section on training towards the end of the book. While it is appreciated that many small firms will not be in a position to employ a trainer initially, its importance cannot be overemphasised. If this is the case for your firm, use the section yourself to enable you to gain maximum results from your staff.

Training is as critical as the job in hand – which is to sell. Selling over the telephone has distinct advantages which we will explore later. It is also a unique form of selling, as it relies totally on the verbal transmission of ideas. The voice alone is mustering the prospect's enthusiasm for the product and prompting him to purchase it. Telephone selling can be an extremely powerful and productive method for businesses to achieve maximum results while ensuring that a good reputation and image are maintained. Use the book as a guideline to set up your own unit, to start your own training sessions or to enhance existing programmes.

The telephone is extremely versatile and can be used either as your only sales tool, or in conjunction with mailshots and brochures, or as a method for making appointments for field sales staff. It can even follow field sales, being utilised to service the account and maximise on continued orders.

Much of what is written in the book may be obvious to you – but then how often do we think of the obvious? I remember being rather puzzled listening to the weather forecasts for one particular summer. A heatwave was promised as evidenced by the frogspawn in the centre of our British ponds. It transpired that as the centre was the last part of the pond to dry out in a drought, this was nature's way of protecting the species. 'Of course,' I thought – an obvious explanation (although it was not a reliable source that year and nature did get it wrong!).

Finally, I must acknowledge my previous employers, Thomson Regional Newspapers. To take a trainee straight from college and show her the basics of sales, training and management was a gamble. Although individualism was strongly encouraged, I could not possibly have written this book without the expertise that was implanted during the years I worked with them. The techniques learned apply to any given situation within an environment built on communication.

To conclude, a thought to ponder. If you really want to do something, you'll find a way. If you don't, you'll find an excuse. If the resources aren't available in-house, look outside. It needn't be expensive; indeed, it could be the most cost-effective investment you'll ever make.

To avoid any misunderstanding, and for that reason alone, the female gender has been used to represent the telesales person and the male for the client.

1 *Creating the right image*

If you want to establish a successful telesales operation the following options are open to you:

1. Recruit an experienced manager and staff.
2. Recruit an experienced manager and let her recruit and train staff.
3. Recruit inexperienced staff and employ an outside agency to train them.
4. Recruit inexperienced staff and train them yourself.

As you know your products and your market better than anyone else, Option 4 is probably the best, but before you can train others, you must perfect the skills of selling over the telephone.

Telephone selling is an art in itself. There is a great deal of skill involved in any type of selling, be it over the phone or face to face on a one-to-one basis, or in a boardroom. Whether following up on an initial enquiry by a customer or making a 'cold call', all salespeople strive to create a professional image. Ask yourself what kind of image you need to create. Words such as 'pleasant', 'positive', 'professional' and 'caring' should all come to mind.

The days of smoothly talking salespeople with 'the gift of the gab' have long gone. Try placing the palm of your hand against a colleague's and take turns applying pressure. What's happening? Generally, the person receiving pressures pushes back so that the hands remain in the same position. In other words, people resist pushiness – automatically. It's innate. Nobody likes being sold to – it takes the power of 'decision making' away. Prospects will, however, be persuaded to buy. The difference is subtle but powerful. Rather like the Grand Master chess player in competition – he thinks each move through and thereby manipulates his opponent's response. It is a matter of control, and feeling in control. Selling is a game – the art of guiding, through carefully planned moves, a potential client into making a favourable decision. I say favourable as the prospect must feel happy with the decision he makes, not coerced but confident that he has made the right move. If this is achieved, the salesperson has won and the right image is projected.

Before looking at aspects of creating this image in detail let us first consider the suitability of your particular product or service to telesales.

Telesales versus field sales

Very often you will hear people say that they don't like using the telephone and that contacting a person face to face is not only much easier but more advantageous. Research has shown that people will retain more information if they have visual contact to support a verbal message. Indeed, up to 55 per cent of our influence in a face-to-face situation is through body language! So why is telephone selling so successful?

While total reliance on verbal message retention has great drawbacks (only up to 85 per cent of what is said is actually taken in), there must be some measure of importance related to retention. For instance, if you are talking to someone over the phone, for example a friend who is interested in the latest bestseller that you have read, then the chances of her retaining all the information are greater because of her personal interest. So then in sales, your well-equipped team will develop the ability to talk to clients about something in which they have skilfully aroused the client's interest. Apart from the voice and skill, very little else is required in telesales. In field sales, however, far more is needed. There are a significant number of disadvantages:

- **Number of calls:** It is not physically possible to visit as many clients as you can phone. A rep would visit up to 15 clients per day but telesales personnel can contact up to 60 clients in that period.
- **Geography:** A route has to be carefully planned to eliminate time-wasting.

- **Decision maker:** If the contact has been unable, at the last minute, to keep the appointment, you will have wasted a call, which is very time-consuming.
- **Desk:** Everything you need will be kept in your briefcase! You cannot afford to forget anything.
- **Appearance:** Clothes, hair, nails, etc all need to be kept neat and tidy – your appearance will be judged, more so than in telesales.
- **Attitude:** You cannot show your disapproval. You must look the client in the eyes and show interest, unlike telesales people, who can frown or shake a fist!
- **Transport:** Reps need to be equipped with cars – very expensive both initially and in running costs, as the cars have to be totally reliable.

Both methods have advantages and disadvantages. You need to consider carefully cost, your product and company needs before making any firm decisions.

Your market

Not all products suit the telephone operation. In essence it is difficult to sell a wholly tangible item, from initial contact to taking the order, over the phone. For instance, if you sell office equipment you wouldn't expect someone to buy it without seeing it first, unless of course they have a brochure. If, however, you sell advertising space, then you are selling an idea and the whole contract can be dealt with over the phone.

The telephone can be used in a number of ways to back up or increase sales, eg by making appointments for your representative to call on the potential client and discuss a purchase. This is still selling, as your telesales person will be persuading the client to spend some of his valuable time with a colleague. Alternatively, the telephone unit can be used to service an existing account as in teleorders. This is a widespread technique and is appropriate when a product, eg confectionery, has been sold to a customer by a representative and a teleorder person phones regularly to take increased or repeat orders, sell new lines, make future appointments if necessary and generally ensure the client is satisfied and has a regular supply of your products.

If your establishment is large enough to set up a call centre, then your operation can become all-electronic, and no paperwork will be necessary (more on this in Chapter 8).

Importance of the voice

The image the customer has of the salesperson is vital. In telesales the image is created through voice alone: there is no smartly dressed representative to see, no glittering product to touch and tantalise – just a voice on the other end of the phone. However good the present telephone system may be, the fact remains that the quality of the sound of the human voice is partially lost through transmission, resulting in the client occasionally misinterpreting your meaning.

Let us now analyse the voice to develop that extra care and attention needed in the process of using the phone.

Clarity

To allow speech to be heard clearly, be careful with your choice of words. Communication is facilitated if you use simple words and easy-to-understand sentences. Avoid jargon and local expressions that may not be easily understood by your clients. Don't sell 'environment observation panels' or 'non-leaking, high-attitude writing sticks' when windows or ballpoint pens are what you mean!

Accents, too, can be a disadvantage, although the uniqueness of your voice is something a prospect can warm to. You don't want to end up sounding like a telephone clone by being too careful and contrived, but you can use an accent to your advantage by speaking clearly and using correct pronunciation – accents can give your message a real boost as they have a unique character and can sound very attractive.

An extremely well-spoken gentleman, placing an advertisement over the phone for a mare, asked the telesales girl to help with the wording. She immediately offered assistance by saying that ads in the horses and ponies section generally started with the size, and asked how many hands high it was. The advertiser replied that it was a mare he was selling. The telesales girl, not wanting to lose face but rather confused, tried another question and asked what colour it was. The client, in a rather exasperated tone said, 'It's green, but I don't see what that has to do with it.' He was in fact selling a lawnmower!

If in doubt spell the name. Accuracy is vital – carelessness can lead to ill feelings. Letters such as Ps and Bs, Ns and Ms, Fs and Ss sound the same over the phone so spell them phonetically. Use this typical list, or make up one of your own.

A	Alpha	N	November
B	Bravo	O	Oscar
C	Charlie	P	Papa
D	Delta	Q	Quebec
E	Echo	R	Romeo
F	Foxtrot	S	Sierra
G	Golf	T	Tango
H	Hotel	U	Uniform
I	India	V	Victor
J	Juliet	W	Whiskey
K	Kilo	X	X-Ray
L	Lima	Y	Yankee
M	Mike	Z	Zulu

Clients will appreciate your concern, and your concern for accuracy will complement your professionalism. This all helps build good customer relations. If your alphabet isn't handy, try making words up yourself. One telesales girl in this situation was trying to spell an unusual word back to a personnel officer for a large company. She got to 'I for ...' and could not think of a word beginning with 'I'; neither could the officer. A few gasps later they came up with 'ink'. This served to mellow the call and there was a mutual understanding as to the importance of accuracy; similarly it broke the ice as it lightened the conversation – although I wouldn't recommend you try this deliberately!

Voice control

- Don't waffle or verbally attack the client like a bull in a china shop. Stop to breathe! Pausing is important.
- Don't speak in a monotone manner; not only does this make you sound boring and unenthusiastic, but it could be misconstrued as meaning that your product is lacking in substance too. Add a little colour to your voice. Expressions are important.
- Relax when you are talking – imagine you were conversing with a new recruit and wanted to stimulate enthusiasm. Verbal

expressions prevent your client missing facial messages and equally importantly they allow you to receive your client's moods and attitudes.

To simplify the meaning of tone in your voice ask the staff you recruit to think of the expression 'oh'. Ask on how many occasions they use it and how it sounds in situations of, for example, surprise, annoyance, acceptance, delight, and so on.

Attitude

Your attitude is magnified over the phone. For instance, if you are uncomfortable you can sound irritable, if you are extremely hearty you can sound intoxicated and if you feel impatient you can sound curt. Relax. Don't rush the call. Take your time and use your sales technique. Remain professional and smile. Yes, a simple smile on the face of a telesales person reflects in the voice and really works. You sound friendly, helpful and caring without being over-familiar. It overcomes a multitude of sins.

Dos and don'ts to aid that professional image

Dos

- **Act naturally:** Remember, your mood is reflected in your voice. Be yourself.
- **Smile:** You will sound pleasant and helpful.
- **Be sincere:** Any detection of insincerity can be catastrophic. Remember, bad word of mouth spreads even more quickly than good.
- **Keep the customer informed:** Remember he can't see you – if you have to turn your attention away from the phone for even a few seconds, tell him, and when you return, apologise for the delay. A few moments on the receiving end of a silent phone can seem like an eternity.
- **Keep relevant information on your desk:** Having prices, facts about your product range, etc to hand will enhance your professionalism.

- **Use the caller's name and identify yourself:** The personal touch adds depth to your call and makes the client feel important, which of course he is. He also knows who he is talking to – people don't like speaking to an unknown source.

Don'ts

- **Keep the customer hanging on:** Be efficient and keep him informed.
- **Obstruct your mouth:** Keep the receiver a few inches away from your mouth to avoid that echoing sound. Don't eat or drink – the sound will be magnified. Have you ever heard anyone exhaling smoke over the phone? It sounds like a hurricane!
- **Talk to colleagues:** Carrying on another conversation is not only rude but may confuse your client.
- **Underestimate your client:** Don't be over-simplistic with your explanations, just keep to the facts and be precise.
- **Make promises you can't keep:** Don't tell him you can deliver on Thursdays just to pacify him when you know you can't. If you ever talk to him again you'll be lucky.
- **Waffle on:** People are interested in their own business, not yours. Explore their past problems and future worries but don't start talking about your own personal experiences.
- **Be negative:** If you're not sure about your products how can you expect your client to be?

The seven Ps

I was taught seven Ps to use in telephone selling. These really work and are all telesales professionals should remember:

1. **Promptness.** Answer the phone immediately. There is nothing worse than holding a receiver listening to the line ringing out. Three rings should be the maximum anyone should have to endure.
2. **Politeness.** Apologise for any delay. A cheerful greeting helps – 'Good morning/afternoon, Jones and Son, may I help you?'
3. **Preparation.** Have information handy – product prices, delivery dates, etc.

4. **Precision.** Be precise and factual. A customer appreciates this more than waffle.
5. **Professionalism**. A customer is interested in his problems, not yours.
6. **Practicality.** Give him what he needs – no one creates an empire overnight and if you encourage your client to take more than he needs you endanger your company's reputation.
7. **Positivity.** Give your client good reasons for buying. Use benefits and get him nodding in agreement. It is very difficult to say no when you're nodding.

Remember – You are never given a second chance to make a first impression!

Although it is not likely that a prospect will decide to buy within the first 30 seconds, he can certainly decide not to buy.

There are many factors that go into making a good first impression. The most important influencing power in good communication is enthusiasm – a word that comes from the Greek '*en theo*', which means 'inner god'. In other words, the capacity to succeed comes from within. If this force is applied correctly (through the right training and guidance), it breeds confidence, which in turn can instil a powerful motivating force in the people with whom we communicate. Enthusiasm encourages positive feedback from customers.

Confidence is also gleaned from knowledge: knowing as much about your product or service – and customer – as you possibly can. This can help to convey credibility and confidence to the customer. It is also important to know why and when customers buy from you – this may be achieved by collecting relevant personal information about your customers.

By far the most powerful way to make a good first impression is to create a rapport. This can only exist when two or more people show harmony – a mutual feeling of well-being and understanding. Next time you sit in a restaurant, watch couples (discreetly, of course!). You'll soon recognise the ones who are getting along well – notice how they look into each other's eyes, angle their heads in the same way, lift their glasses simultaneously. When one begins to eat, the other does as well and with the same sort of movement – they are mirroring one another. But it often isn't just their body language. They may speak in the same tone, use the same vocabulary and phraseology, even pause in the same rhythm – this pacing demonstrates rapport.

To cultivate a rapport over the phone, you must use open and honest conversation, listening carefully to the voice, sound and content of the prospect's answers and questions. Meet him on his own level to make him feel at ease. Think about the skills and techniques you must develop so you can achieve this without sounding insincere or patronising. A pattern will begin to emerge. Like-minded people mix together. Rapport is based on mutual respect. You both need to relate to each other, but *you* are the one who is going to have to engineer the process. The differences and similarities between you will emerge fairly quickly. If you become negative, you will merely highlight those differences in the customer's mind. By remaining positive, you are concentrating on the similarities between you. Concentrating your efforts in this way will develop an understanding that will help you to bond.

However, we cannot agree with everything or we will lose our credibility. But we do want to show we understand. By mirroring or duplicating actions or statements, we show that we see and share the other person's very real hopes, fears, worries, expectations, etc. To be agreeable is not condescending, but shows true empathy – meeting people on their own ground so that they feel in unison with us. By mastering the technique you'll find you can engage your customer in a favourable way.

The two key areas in mirroring over the phone are: 1) *voice mirroring* through pitch, tone, pacing, vocabulary, phraseology, tempo, etc; and 2) *emotional mirroring* through attitude, belief, tolerance, understanding, compatibility through respect, involvement, sharing qualities, etc. Your personality and the way you relate to the customer can help influence the impression you give. For example, if you are in an organisation that provides a product or service identical to that supplied by another firm, why would a prospect choose to buy from you over the direct competition? The answer, quite simply, is because of you. *You* are the company, product, service. How you relate to the customer will largely determine the results of the call. In conclusion then: how you view the customer will reflect how you yourself are viewed.

2

Be prepared

If you were to hold a dinner party, how would you go about arranging it? A good host/ess will tell you that to hold a successful dinner party, a great deal of planning is necessary. Compatibility of guests, seating arrangements, lighting, music, menu (including guests' special diets, if any), drinks, dress, timing, etc are all important.

Preparing yourself to handle telephone calls is just as vital. If you have ever tried to simply pick up that receiver and speak then you'll understand why. Preparation for telesales can be categorised into two key areas: first, through emotional and mental attitude, and secondly, with factual information.

Emotional/mental attitude

Getting into the right frame of mind is not as easy as it sounds. Some people seem to be, and are, naturally self-motivated. Highly motivated people often have clear personal goals which they seek to achieve through their performance. The key to motivation, quite simply, is inspiration. There is a saying that you are paid to do a job of work and so you should do it to the best of your ability, but there is a great deal more to motivation than monetary reward.

People will ill-defined goals are less able to identify with their work and this obviously reduces effort. Take time to analyse the purpose of one of your calls. What do you hope to achieve? By having specific aims, you, as an individual, are more able to measure your performance. Recognising well-defined goals increases self-motivation and enthusiasm. We looked at the importance of enthusiasm earlier and the positive feedback it generates. When you eventually recruit staff, allow them to discuss in groups the importance of selling goals. By realising their significance they become motivated to set goals; by assessing their call they will become more proficient and achieve company targets; by being successful they will become more enthusiastic and self-motivated; and so on. (See Figure 2.1.)

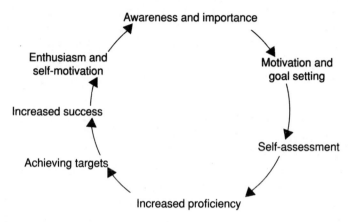

Figure 2.1 The motivation cycle

All this leads to building confidence. Without self-confidence the salesperson will be unable to instil enthusiasm and confidence in the prospect.

No matter how experienced telesales personnel are in worldly affairs, a customer is interested only in his own problems. Avoid competing with him in the knowledge test. No matter how subtle, the result is still oneupmanship.

First man:	'I had a dreadful cold and was ill for several days.'
Second man:	'Oh, I had flu, it was awful.'
First man:	'Actually I had pleurisy.'
Second man:	'My flu was so bad I ended up in hospital with pneumonia.'
First man:	'Oh, I went to hospital and I died there.'

The above sounds ridiculous, but it does illustrate the dangers. It is best to understand the client's problems and lend a sympathetic ear but refrain from giving personal views or experiences, unless of course invited.

Factual information

Product/prices/competitors

Knowing your own product and prices is of paramount importance obviously, but do you know as much about your competitors? Knowing your rivals in the market helps keep you one step ahead. If your prospect or potential client is unsure who to use or buy from, you will have the advantage because you will understand why he is having difficulties in reaching a decision. With this knowledge you can highlight the benefits of your company to help sway the result in your favour. Belief in your product is equally important – if *you* are convinced you are more likely to convince your client.

Testimonials

Keep records of other clients who have used you successfully and keep updating the information when you talk to your regular customers. This is solid evidence. By relaying factual information to potential clients about the successes of your other clients, who may well be their competitors, they are more likely to buy, as any doubts will have been removed and your credibility increased. 'If it works for J B Ltd there is no reason why it shouldn't work for you, is there?'

Questions

If the information prospects give is vague, ask searching questions to find out more. The questions should be open-ended and start with 'Why', 'How', 'When', 'Where' and 'Whom'. You are unlikely to succeed in selling if you have limited information. Prepare questions that will give you the information you need.

Objections

Anticipate reasons why prospects may decide not to buy from you:

- **New customer:** Possibly cost; very often objections are cost related.
- **Existing client:** Possibly had difficulties with deliveries from you and needs reassuring.

Objections will be handled in detail in Chapter 6. Remember, though, that your call will be more fluent if you have anticipated any possible objections.

Information pointers, scripts or word tracks

Because telesales people cannot be seen, they can write down key points and refer to them. This reference enables you to stress important facts without the fear of eliminating vital information. Information pointers should contain guideline questions, presentation points, selling phrases and closes. Many firms use complete sales scripts, but they can threaten your credibility by making you sound like a parrot. More importantly though, when a customer asks a question or objects, he throws the call into chaos because you are not prepared or ready and the script doesn't allow for interruptions. By charading (role-playing the part) first you can help avoid any embarrassing moments. Not only will it help to build your confidence in the use of sales techniques but it will enable you to become more selective and skilled with the material you draw from the pointer. If you use information pointers correctly, you will appreciate their flexibility. For instance, when a client asks a question and interrupts the flow, he can be drawn back to the key points or to areas not yet covered. As it is impossible to rely 100 per cent on memory, information pointers can be used as a stepping stone in ensuring that a completely professional and comprehensive presentation is delivered (see Figure 2.2). Not all the information prepared will be significant in every call, so you can select the appropriate points.

Know your client

What do people buy? Take two descriptions for the same holiday destination written by two separate travel companies.

Company 1: 'Take a break this summer and treat yourself to a holiday of a lifetime – Bali.'

Company 2: 'Bali – beautiful, breathtaking, bountiful and blessed. Nothing is ordinary – the lushness of the trees and flowers, the beautiful protected beaches and the gentle artistic people. A holiday filled with festivals and exotic island feasts under the brilliant stars. Now you can believe in paradise.'

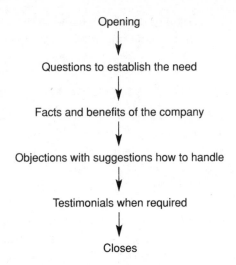

Figure 2.2   Structure of the information pointer

Company 2 has the greater response because the description satisfies human desires: it is aspirational. People buy a product or service to satisfy a certain need. Whether the product is something they want or not is largely irrelevant, as decisions will be made only once the 'what's in it for me' syndrome has been clarified. It is only natural that we look to our own comfort, success, security and profitability first. The salesperson who sells purely the product and what it is, rather than what it does, will not succeed.

The features or selling points of the products are manufactured qualities, ie *what it is*. Such features are inherent from the time of making and nothing will change that, eg 'This car has cloth upholstery.' The benefits or advantages are what can be derived from the features, ie what it does or 'what's in it for me?'. The benefit of the cloth upholstery, then, is that it is comfortable. In order to persuade people to buy, the telesales person must consider what benefits her product/service offers. She must know not only her product but the advantages the product offers to her client. As clients' needs often vary, the telesales person, by asking searching questions (discussed in more detail in Chapter 4), will be able to tailor specific benefits to particular clients' needs to fulfil them. In other words, by linking what your product can do, with what your clients want done. In conclusion to the importance of preparation, remember this simple motto:

Nobody plans to fail, they just fail to plan.

3 *Incoming calls and how to handle them*

If we don't take care of the customer, someone else will. A telesales person is the representative of a company. Although the role is primarily one of selling, it also entails public relations. When you take that receiver in your hand to answer a call, you do so without knowing who you will be talking to, or what their purpose is. It could be a general enquiry, a price query, a customer wanting a repeat order or even a complaint. Whatever the reason, the caller will expect to be handled correctly. Apart from value for money, a person expects efficiency and sound professional advice.

Complaints

By handling complaints properly you can actually turn the call into more business. Following this simple guideline can help you to do just that.

Telesales staff are the people who receive complaints calls, but complaints are usually directed at the company, so don't take it personally. The caller needs to get it off his chest, so listen carefully and take down the information he gives you. Ask open questions if you need more information, recap to make sure you have all the relevant points and then decide on a plan of action. Without taking sides, empathise and tell the customer what you intend to do and get his agreement (he can't then complain about your decision). Once he has agreed, carry the plan out. Check that it has been done and once you are satisfied phone the client back to confirm it.

If you're not in a position to handle the complaint and the decision needs to come from a higher authority, don't make any rash promises. Keep the caller advised, tell him who he needs to speak to and arrange for him to be phoned back.

Complaints should be logged so that managers can see what type of complaints they get – this is useful for showing up any weaknesses in the company's system. They also show if any particular staff receive more than others – perhaps there is an administration problem with a specific person – so that training to rectify the situation can be implemented.

Types of people

People's attitudes vary enormously, as do their natures. Less easily manageable people can be placed into five main types: shy, forgetful, aggressive, talkative and knowledgeable.

Shy

Shyness or fear are the most common obstacles to successful communication. In studies up to 40 per cent of people describe themselves as shy, while a further 15 per cent of the population are 'situationally shy' – that is, they experience shyness in stressful situations. Many find the telephone stressful. Just because shy people are usually less aggressive than most, that doesn't mean they are any less important. It is probably easier to lose custom from these people as they are often afraid to air their views or ask you to repeat something they have misheard or misunderstood. Be tactful and try to draw information from them by asking how they feel about your product, their customers, etc and why. Listen to what they have to say and where applicable flatter them on their decisions or thoughts, or quote other clients who have similar views. Drawing information helps to build a shy person's confidence and will help to ease the burden of communication. You will find that your skill in handling shy people will have succeeded when they start asking you questions. If they become confident enough to request more information from you, then you have achieved your aim.

Forgetful

It is infuriating to receive a call from someone who has forgotten essential facts, but if you're honest, you will recall times when you have needed reminding about something. Be patient. It could be that your client has misunderstood something and needs clarification but is afraid of appearing ignorant. Gently remind him of the points and reassure him that you are grateful for the call and understand the importance of his concern for getting it right.

Aggressive

A telesales person, minding her own business, working hard and well, answers the phone to receive verbal abuse. Perhaps the client's order has been stopped because through the negligence of the accounts department he has been wrongly labelled a 'bad debtor'. Obviously this is a case you would hope never to experience: nevertheless such a situation does occur. The client would have every reason to be angry and may have lost much of his own valuable time and business custom because of this. Initially the caller will channel his aggressions towards the telesales person as she is the representative of the company. Follow the rules for handling complaints mentioned earlier: don't take it personally and listen to what he has to say. There is absolutely no point in interrupting the call – even if he is speaking to the wrong person. The silent technique allows the customer to let off steam and you to collate your thoughts. Once you are allowed to speak, by which time he is probably feeling slightly remorseful at having steered all his aggression to you, answer sympathetically but with sincerity. Be calm but professional, tell him you understand how he must feel without putting the blame on anyone (especially remain loyal to your company) and tell him what you intend to do and do it. If you can't solve the problem, ensure that someone who can, phones him back. If the customer turns out to be mistaken, never declare yourself the winner – he as the loser will resent this. You should remain sympathetic, showing that you can understand the reasons for his error, but point to the facts.

Some people become aggressive when they don't understand something – it can be likened to a safety mechanism – or when they are asked searching questions. Apologise but explain the necessity of the questions so that you may ascertain which particular range of your product would suit him best as you are sure that he doesn't want to buy anything that isn't actually totally suitable. He will respect this and usually help with his answers.

Talkative

Few people actually admit that they value their own importance and opinions primarily. Yet given the chance, most of us could talk indefinitely about our experiences, expectations in life, successes and failures. If you have asked a client for information (some people don't even need that as an excuse!) it may be difficult, once you have established the need, or even sold the product, to get him off the line. Take a deep breath and remain polite but firm. Point out that he is obviously very busy, as you are, so you won't detain him any longer but that you look forward to continuing the conversation another time. Thank him for the call and get off the line. Initially this tactic may feel alien but it does work, so practise using it.

Knowledgeable

The final category is someone who knows it all, or at least thinks he does. He could run his company blindfold (and probably yours, given the chance) so who are you to tell him what's what? Again, remain calm, then flatter his expertise, following it up with a testimonial. 'Being an astute businessman', he would probably be interested to hear how his competitors, who buy from you, are doing because of it. You are allowing him to withdraw his attitude gracefully and he will admire your integrity.

The customer

One of the main advantages of a customer phoning in is that he is doing so in a buying frame of mind. At this stage he may only be ringing around for price quotes; nevertheless, you have the opportunity to speak to him. You will need to sound professional, positive, caring and efficient – qualities attained as one's selling skills are developed. Think of an actor who performs on stage and receives the applause of an appreciative audience. He gains this because he has learned his lines and rehearsed his part under the guidance of the director. Telesales personnel too need nurturing. We have already looked at the importance of image over the phone and how a client may perceive a telesales person's attitude through voice alone. A potential client is phoning you in order to communicate. It is the task of the salesperson to maintain the conversation – without it there is a real danger that no sale will be made as communication dwindles. Word pointers are extremely useful as they prompt you, first, into conversing successfully, and secondly, into establishing relevant details about the customer and his needs. By practising and charading the techniques you can learn to put your own personality into the areas to be covered. This not only develops your confidence as you become more familiar and at ease with the implementation, but also prevents you from talking 'parrot-fashion' through an obvious lack of training.

Any individual who has tailored the techniques to suit her personality through using guideline scripts will have done so without changing the sequence or losing any of the important benefits. Take a livery stable that the owner knows to be superior. Once prospects have seen the stable and surroundings, they usually place their booking. People often ring the owner to compare prices with other stables. She can either give the prices outright and chance losing them or she can use a carefully prepared question like 'Most of my clients prefer to see the livery before they make any decisions; when would be convenient for you to call?' She knows that the welfare of the horses is vital to the prospect and is showing that she has nothing to hide. She is inviting him to be selective, and even if he insists on a price there and then, he will remember her comment and probably return to see the stables.

To start the call and to maximise on all selling opportunities a telesales person should begin the call with enthusiasm: 'Good morning/afternoon, Blockins Garden Company. May I help you?' The purpose is threefold: it offers a cheerful greeting, an acknowledgement that the correct number has been dialled and an offer of assistance. The prospect will automatically reveal the purpose of his call:

Prospect:	'I want some information about garden sheds.'
Telesales person:	'You're through to the right person, my name is Sofia, you are…?'
Prospect:	'Mr Daniels.'
Telesales person:	'How may I help you, Mr Daniels?'
Prospect:	'I want to price your garden sheds.'

At this stage the girl has the prospect's name and is using it to break the formality. She does not yet know whether or not the prospect is phoning other centres and comparing prices. Assuming this garden centre stocks a large range of sheds, questions need to be asked to ascertain what type of shed is required and what price range will suit the prospect. Although people will buy what is best for them, don't go mad with the idea and sell the top end of the range if you know that a less expensive shed will serve the purpose. You're not in the trade to 'con' the public although you are competitive and don't want to under-sell either – or worse still, lose the prospect to a competitor. So you need more information:

Telesales person: 'What do you intend using it for, Mr Daniels?'

This open question helps the telesales person establish whether the shed is for commercial or private use and whether a larger, stronger or smaller shed would be suitable. She also ends the question with the prospect's name, ie adding the personal touch and showing that he is important.

Occasionally the prospect may resent questions – he may have a preconceived idea of the size of the shed he needs. Do not become disconcerted. Explain that you are asking these questions to find out which type of shed would be best suited to his needs. He obviously does not want anything that is unsuitable. Remember too that you cannot start talking about the benefits of your products until you have established the need. For your product to become a benefit there must be a need, and it is the telesales person's task to establish these needs through selective questioning: 'What are you looking for in a washing machine?'; 'Which part of your house faces north?'; 'How often do you cater for large numbers?'; 'What type of machinery do you use?' etc. The questions will lead to a need as long as you listen to the answers. You then need to clarify the situation by restating your findings so that the client knows what's what:

Telesales person: 'So as I see it, Mrs Smith, you are looking for a microwave with a built-in browning device that is large enough to cater for a family of six without having too many extras, is that right?'

The clarification is ended with a question so that the client can confirm with a 'yes'. If the answer is 'no', then you ask more questions to find the right need. If 'yes', then you have arrived at the selling stage and now have the opportunity to tell the prospect about your product. Avoid phrases like 'I advise' or 'I recommend' as your personal feelings are irrelevant. Your presentation of the product should be filled with relevant facts and carefully selected benefits and remain totally professional. Enthusiasm is infectious, so ensure you know your product inside out and use your information pointer.

Imagine, then, that you have established that your prospect is looking for an office desk for himself at his new offices, which are housed in a large Georgian building. Size is no obstacle as the rooms are large and spacious. The firm is a prestigious one and image is important. Having seen your brochure, he phones you:

Telesales person: 'We have recently started stocking Xmar products, which are renowned for their quality and value. This means that you will possess a prestigious desk, Mr Jones, which is in keeping with your position and company image. Part of the range is in reproduction style. The mahogany would be especially suitable for you as the decor of the Georgian era lends itself to this wood and so it would be in keeping with the environment. The desktops are covered in leather, which is traditional of the style. This obviously protects the desk surface so that while you enjoy its luxury you can be assured of its durability. The desk combines quality with practicality and luxury for just £XXXX and comes complete with an executive leather swivel chair which is exclusive to Xmar products. In all, it gives significant support to your reputation, Mr Jones, which is obviously important, isn't it?

Do not pause here, but go into the close:

Telesales person: 'The leather comes in honey, green or red. Which would you prefer?'
Prospect: 'Red.'
Telesales person: 'Fine, we deliver in your area on Thursdays. What time would be convenient for you?'

A good telesales person will carry this off with conviction. Naturally, objections do occur at times and this is covered in Chapter 6. The example above is fairly straightforward. However, just because a client phones in with a particular item in mind (which could be on impulse or as a response to an advertisement or mailshot), that doesn't mean that he needs only that item. During the questioning stage the telesales person should find out if the client has any other requirements – in this example, what other office equipment or furniture does he require? Maximise on everything. Your thoughtfulness (provided it is not pressurised) will be appreciated as prospects will have a limited knowledge of the extent of your range.

Some clients will not buy at the enquiry stage – remember, don't be forceful. Nobody likes to feel they are being pushed. Remain professional and give the benefits. If you extend your advice but leave the door open, the client may well come back. He will certainly remember your caring attitude and expertise.

The important factor in selling is that a conversation takes place between the telesales person and the prospect. The extent of the effectiveness of selling skills will be mirrored in the success of the salesperson. The process of persuading people to buy lies not only in the techniques used but also in the skill with which they have been taught. Many organisations start recruits on a telesales career by getting them to handle incoming calls. As familiarity with the group and its systems develops, so staff awareness and knowledge grows. Training is indispensable, but theory alone, even charades, does not lead wholly to achievements. Practical experience, as in any profession, is vital. When you recruit staff, time should be allocated, preferably each week, when sales staff can get together and discuss the calls they have handled. No matter how successful and confident a salesperson may be, knowledge and understanding is accelerated when group analysis is available. As no two clients or salespeople are the same, each can learn from the other's experiences.

The key to successful communication lies in a structural balance between talking and listening. Two psychologists structured communication using the method shown in Table 3.1.

1. *Open.* There are areas within your business that both you and your clients know, eg the name of the company, what it provides, etc. This is the 'open' area.
2. *Hidden.* Your customers do not know some areas, though. These

Table 3.1   Forms of communication

	You know	You don't know
Others know	*Open*	*Blind*
Others don't know	*Hidden*	*Unknown*

    are hidden and may include price increases, openings of new premises, etc.

3. *Blind.* Some clients have heard things that we don't know about. Perhaps a new business in direct competition with your company has approached them for custom or an independent source has commented about your company. Or maybe the customer's circumstances have changed. This is the 'blind' area.

4. *Unknown.* This covers aspects of the business that are unknown to both parties, and could include reactions to the fall in the pound sterling, a new government coming into office, etc.

What Table 3.1 demonstrates is that if we consider all possibilities, we can extract enough information to develop rapport. The two key areas to expand on are the 'hidden' and 'blind' areas. Your ability to develop good communication here will depend on your questioning and listening skills. The more we ask, the more feedback we receive and the more enlightened we become. Similarly, the more relevant information we give our customers, the greater their understanding of how we can help and best serve them. The challenge is to keep improving the service levels.

4 Improving your cold calls

Who and how?

Your regular clients and incoming calls, to an extent, probably generate your 'bread and butter' income, but inevitably this alone will not achieve company targets. Targets are carefully planned from budget forecasts to allow firms to enter the realms of profit. How, then, are you going to set about winning that extra business? You will need to expand your client list and to do this you need to contact new prospects. It is called *cold calling*. This chapter aims to help you in the planning stage of gaining new business.

In recent years there have been changes in the law, designed to help protect consumers. At the end of Chapter 7, I have included some 'essentials' to assist you in taking account of these changes.

Prospecting

All businesses aim for profit – if this goal were not achieved they would fold very quickly. In order to compete for new clients and gain your share in the marketplace, you must expand your clientele. To do this you need to find new leads and contact new prospects. But how? It is clear that only a certain proportion of the population will need your product or service. Of these, only a minority will have an urgent and immediate need that you can satisfy. The remainder may need you but either that requirement isn't a priority or they don't realise it yet. It is these two types, subject to your abilities at cold calling, that will buy. So who are these people that you are going to get business from and how will you find them?

Existing accounts

You will, presumably, be constantly finding ways of asking for additional orders – whether supplying existing clients with products that they have been buying elsewhere or increasing their existing orders. Through your questioning you should be continually exploring their past problems and future concerns. Include their competitors in this. Ask who they feel are a threat and whom they perceive they threaten. You will gain knowledge to help you with your existing clients' orders and to discover names of organisations that you were not aware of, or new companies that may wish to do business with you.

Personal observations

Valuable leads can be obtained from directories (whether industrial or telephone), advertisements in trade catalogues, specialist magazines, brochures, local and national press (including job advertisements). Editorial stories are also a strong source of revelation, as is television. Any trade associations, trade organisation or local authority can provide valuable leads. This area is endless – even passing by a new site you can discover who is building or who will be moving into the premises. Keep your eyes and ears open. Get your friends to ask around – they too have a role to play. For more useful information on acquiring external leads, try contacting the Direct Marketing Association UK (contact details given on page 72).

Preparation

You have an abundance of leads and it's time to start calling – or is it? I outlined the importance of careful planning earlier. Much of that planning will be used in 'cold calling', but now you have the advantage of knowing who you are calling – use that advantage and do a little research. Your brain is the world's most original computer; the software needs to contain the answers to the following questions:

- How will the prospect gain from the sale?
- What will he lose by not buying?
- Do I have relevant open-ended questions to draw the need?
- Do I have enough relevant information to satisfy his needs and will all the points be covered in correct sequence?
- Am I prepared to tailor the benefits to his specific needs and relay them in such a way that they mean something to him?

- If he objects, will I be able to handle the objections shrewdly?
- Will I be able to answer his questions accurately?
- Can I back up my convictions with testimonials?
- Am I prepared to spot buying signals and close the sale?

Preparation is as important as the sale itself. You cannot rely on luck. You need hard graft and determination, quality preparation and a sales technique that is handled with finesse. Armed with this material, you will have a greater chance of success.

The art of listening

Unless somebody listens to the message and understands it, there is no communication, only noise! If you are too anxious to put your point across you may not hear vital clues. Listening is non-verbal communication and complements questions. It is a listening skill to acknowledge the person who is talking and to keep the conversation going. It shows approval of what the other person is saying.

Talking alone will not win results. Conversation is your initial aim. To establish two-way communication you need rapport; she who fails to listen to the responses of others not only will appear ignorant but may miss vital clues or signals. Listen to the client, take notes – this will help you to remember the important points. Remember to be selective though. Questions prepared in advance should free your mind for listening – don't, in your eagerness, race through your information pointer like a bull in a china shop. If you feel you have misunderstood a point, ask your prospect to clarity it; by clearing it up now you will avoid embarrassment later. When you refer to the notes you have made, and you wish to pursue a thought, start the sentence with phrases like 'you said' or 'you mentioned earlier'. You can use these points then to reflect on an important area, clarify a point or lead to another open-ended question. Allow your prospect time to answer and never interrupt him or anticipate what he is going to say – not only is it rude to finish someone's sentence, but it is distracting to the prospect's thought process. Invariably prospects will object with 'red herrings' (more in Chapter 6). These may seem irrational, but don't be distracted and become mentally argumentative. Nor be distracted by anything in your working environment. Concentrate on what the customer is saying.

Authority

A customer picks up the phone to be greeted cheerfully by 'Hello, Mr Hall, it's Janice here. I'm ringing to let you know that this is your lucky week because I can save you £500.'

All very well, but this girl has broken several golden rules in one opening sentence. Let's assume Janice is selling double glazing. Having opened a local directory she dials the number.

1. She assumes that Mr Hall still lives there. People do move from time to time and it's not worth gambling that you have the right name straight off.
2. It is a fact that many people are wary of speaking to an unknown source. Janice didn't say where she was from or what company she represented. Although it would have become apparent quite quickly that she was representing a double glazing firm, she would have instigated animosity because her opening was vague and misleading.
3. Why is the man so lucky when the privacy of his home life has been intruded upon?

Telesales personnel selling to the private market have to be especially careful when phoning prospects because they generally have to phone out of office hours when the family are together and also because individuals often prefer to initiate the search for purchases themselves. This is true too of business executives, but being in a more commercial environment they are more likely to lend an ear.

Having decided who to call, preparing and ascertaining as far as possible that the prospect is creditworthy, the telesales person should start the call very differently. Janice would have been much safer saying, 'Hello, is that Mr Hall?' It is important that you speak to the correct person – the buyer or decision maker. A call to a business from, say, a staff agency could be 'Hello, this is Sally James from the Business Recruitment Agency. Could you give me the name of the personnel officer, please?' A telesales person representing a manufacturing company calling a wholesaler or retailer could say 'Hello, this is Julia Armitage from Visions, would you tell me who it is that handles the buying for your fashion section/department, please?' You are far more likely to receive the information you need because the questions lend themselves to favourable answers. By nature few people are deliberately rude to or ignorant of others. Once you have the name, write it down – you will need to use the client's name to add that personal touch. So far so good. Now speak to that person:

Telesales person: 'I see, would you put me through to Mrs Roberts please.'

Sometimes you are put straight through, but there will be many occasions when you are put through to the secretary (or receptionist, in the case of smaller firms). Secretaries are said to be the nightmare of salespeople, reducing their confidence to worry. This should not happen. Once telesales people realise that secretaries have a job to do like anyone else, and may be under strict instructions to vet calls before putting them through, then they can be handled.

We know that trying to sell to anyone other than the decision maker is a waste of time. By the time the message has been relayed it is second-hand and a secretary will not have the same convictions and techniques as the telesales person. It is important, however, to keep on the right side of the secretary/receptionist. She has the power to put you through and can become an important ally in the future. She may also one day become the decisions makers herself, and if ill-treated by you now she will remember.

Secretary: 'Hello, Mr Quinn's secretary.'
Telesales person: 'Hello, this is Rosemary Brown from Jacksons Ltd. May I speak to Mr Quinn, please?'
Secretary: 'What is it in connection with?'

That last dreaded question can be easily overcome by the telesales person remaining calm, professional and understanding of the secretary's position and the reason for her question. You and she both know that she is not the decision maker, so clarify this.

Telesales person: 'Well, we manufacture metal sheeting as you probably know and I understand Mr Quinn is in charge of the supplies. Is he there?'

The secretary knows you are a salesperson because you have given her a snippet of information and accepts that while you are sensitive to her role you do need to speak to Mr Quinn or someone else in authority.

What is especially interesting, though, is that because you have ended the sentence with a question she is forced to answer:

Secretary:	'Well, he's in a meeting right now.'
Telesales person:	'When would be a good time to call back?'
Secretary:	'After lunch.'
Telesales person:	'Around 2 pm?'
Secretary:	'Fine.'
Telesales person:	'I'll call back at 2 pm then, thank you for your help.'

The telesales person has remained in command and not allowed any uncomfortable pauses. In doing so she has ascertained a convenient time for the secretary to transfer the call. Because the secretary gave this information and arranged the appointment she will be obliged to put you through when you call back. Make sure that you do ring back on time, or if you are unable to, get someone to do it for you. Other secretaries may ask, 'Can I help?' Again, remembering the rules of harmony, keep within their confines and say 'Yes you can' (confirming their importance). 'My director has asked me to phone your boss; perhaps you can tell me when he'll be free and I'll call back?' This will either force her to give a time to call back or lead her to the 'What is it in connection with?' which we have just covered. It is significant that by treating a secretary in this way you will develop a mutual understanding and respect. No two calls will be the same. Learning in this way is invaluable and the more practised and familiar you are, the more fluent and spontaneous will be the response. The absolute rejection by some secretaries can be disconcerting, however, so the trick is to recognise a glimmer of interest. This glimmer may not be obvious to the untrained ear but practice helps!

Once, while on a mission impossible, ie selling the unsellable to the unconvinced, I happened upon one of those protective secretaries who told me that under no circumstances would her boss be remotely interested. Finally, when she agreed to call me back in the unlikely event of Mr Big feeling it was worthwhile, it transpired that we shared the same extension number. This, of all things, caught her imagination. Naturally I shared in her wonderment. Developing a relationship based on three digits is not easy, but at last we had found a common interest! That part was pot luck, but everyone can learn to turn the unlikely into an eventual sale.

Now that the groundwork has been covered, your staff are ready to follow the selling techniques. The internationally recognised pattern of a sale developed in the United States many years ago is as follows:

A – **A**ttention
I – **I**nterest
D – **D**esire
A – **A**ction

Quite simply it means that the salesperson must arouse the prospect's favourable *attention* to stimulate his persona*l interest* in your product. Then, by identifying benefits, the prospect sees the product as *desirable* and is manoeuvred to take the necessary *action* to purchase it. The remainder of this chapter will examine the AIDA pattern in some detail.

The introduction and warm-up

Many firms send out mailshots to precede calls. It is largely a personal matter, although certain products need to be seen before they can be sold. However, the follow-up calls could follow the said AIDA pattern.

Attention

First impressions count. We all know this to be true and so the strength of the opening of the sale is of paramount importance. Think of your prospect – he is probably a busy who is tied up in the everyday running of his company when you phone. A conversation with you about your products is likely to be furthest from his mind. How then are you going to get his favourable attention? 'I've got some information about one of our new lines that I know you'll be interested in' is not going to establish two-way communication. The prospect will withdraw immediately. When you watch a film or go to a concert, you usually know within the first few minutes whether it is going to be compelling. The same applies in sales. The customer listens more carefully to the first sentence than to any other – by doing so he is able to decide whether he is going to listen or terminate the conversation. Put yourself in the customer's shoes, emphasise and ask yourself what it would take to arouse your attention in his situation. Your customer requires a skilled and stimulating approach to allow his attention to be diverted from his own self-interest to you. Prepare single questions that would arouse his attention in any given situation. Asking questions that involve the customer is imperative but if they are not posed correctly they will make your task more difficult.

A security systems telesales person who starts with 'Would you be interested in buying a burglar alarm?' leaves herself wide open for a negative response. A better approach would be: 'Burglary has increased by 10 per cent over the last 12 months: when was the last time you heard of a house robbed locally?' By focusing the question on the prospect's own environment and quoting national figures (which must be accurate) she has encouraged him to think. Something that is close to home will increase his awareness of the need for personal home security and stimulate his attention.

Openings can be posed in a variety of ways and can invite response for a variety of reasons. Below are three of the more popular tried-and-tested methods, which can be accepted depending on your product or service and whether the customer is regular or a new prospect.

Knowledge

This may be used to give the customer information which is applicable, or of particular interest, to him. It could be evidence that another of your clients is doing well through you, by using a testimonial or a current news item:

> I have just been speaking to J J Factories who installed our new lighting system twelve months ago. They say that absenteeism has been reduced by 5 per cent because their machinists no longer complain of poor eyesight or headaches. I thought of you immediately as I know how important good staff working conditions are to you.

or

> Have you heard that planning permission is being sought by your competitors RMA at the Exeter compound?

Alternatively use it as a request for information from your prospect. A recruitment agency speaking to personnel officers may ask, 'How much of your valuable time is spent on interviewing possible candidates?' *and* 'What percentage of first interviewees do you have back for seconds?', *or* a more general request for information to a retailer: 'What are your most popular lines, Mr Jones?'

Observation

This kind of opening is based on the knowledge that you have gained from a previous conversation with the prospect but were unable to pinpoint or overcome at that time. Having thought about the information you have been given, you simply go back to the prospect, making reference to the previous call, with any ideas. A computer software telesales person may have been too keen to promote the cost-saving element of her organisation's product without really listening to the client's answers. Perhaps the prospect was more concerned about spending less time with his staff, which he feared would result from buying new devices. The observation will allow the telesales person to recapture that fear and step in with a second chance:

> Last time we spoke, you expressed your concern over the amount of time you spend away from your staff. How would you like to be in a position where you could spend even more time keeping in personal contact with them?

The prospect will listen because he can relate. The opening is geared to his immediate personal interest and the telesales person is then in a position to explain how this software could actually save him administrative time and give him time to spend with his staff. Alternatively, a company previously without finance arrangements that subsequently brings in a loan scheme would then be in a position to go back to clients who were afraid of cost:

> I've been thinking about our last discussion regarding finance and I am now in a position to help. More people are benefiting from our products now, by taking advantage of our new finance facilities.

Complimentary remarks

In order to pay someone a compliment or to flatter them you must be sincere. Insincerity is easily spotted and sounds churlish. Compliments can be paid in various ways: 'I've been admiring your new logo, Mr

Hall. Tell me, did you design it or did you get someone to do it for you?' Or less directly: 'You have a reputation for being the most fashionable boutique in town.' The client will be flattered by your interest and give you an answer.

In the latter case, the telesales person is preparing the prospect to buy fashion earrings.

The complimentary opening can also be used in a more subtle way, by asking the client's opinion – the fact that you have asked for his views will flatter him. A client from a confectionary company that may be selling sweets to kiosks and cinemas could be asked, 'How, in your opinion, has the unemployment crisis affected business in the entertainment industry?' Regardless of the answer, the telesales person can go on to talk about the importance of the public enjoying themselves and pampering their 'naughty but nice' side by having a good selection of confectionery to choose from. The question is posed in such a way that you are not asking the prospect to give you any information about his own business, which may be suffering, as he is unlikely to admit that to a stranger. By asking his advice about his type of business you are taking the pressure off him and his answer will be mirroring his own cinema or shop anyway.

We all like compliments; they boost our egos and can make us susceptible. Your prospect is exactly the same: few are immune to flattery. Your prospect is the expert in his business and can tell you a great deal about the marketplace. When you open the sale you are not only arousing attention but are enticing the prospect to communicate, which leads to his listening to what you have to say and offer.

Interest

Your aim is to establish the need of the client. Earlier we looked at buying trends – people buy what is best for them. To sell you have to show the client what he's buying – he's buying benefits. In order to be selective with benefits and gear them to a prospect's need you have to establish what that need is. Guessing is not enough. The psychology in establishing communication favourably is twofold:

1. Drawing information from the client (answers to questions which you have construed in your preparation) in a way that makes him aware of his own needs. If he's not convinced your product can help, he will resist your sale.

2. By asking questions you strive to involve your prospect in conversation. By answering he will automatically be more communicative while relaying vital information.

There are two types of questions. Those of the first type are searching, *open-ended questions* that begin with 'How', 'Why', 'When', 'Where' and 'Whom' which encourage a full answer. For example. find out 'why' they feel the way they do, 'what' they are looking for, 'how' they think the situation could be remedied and 'when' they have in mind (ie a deadline). The second type are *closed questions* which require a 'Yes/No' answer and start with 'Do you', 'Have you', etc. It is also sensible to avoid the present tense so that the prospect doesn't have to relate to current failures if they exist and won't feel you are prying or that he is being pressurised. Questions posed to explore a prospect's past problems and future worries are much more fruitful, provided, of course, you listen to the answers!

Open-ended questions

- 'Where, in the past, have you found the majority of your customers come from?'
- 'What has been your best-selling line?'
- 'Which days have you found are your busiest?'
- 'How have most of your customers paid for goods – cash or by credit card?'

Closed questions

- 'Do you provide a delivery service?'
- 'Do you accept credit cards?'
- 'Have you ever stocked other lines?'
- 'Do you sell water colours?'

Once you have listened to the answers to the questions and taken notes, you can suggest ways in which he can be helped by buying your product. The number of questions you need to ask varies. It's like 'How long is a ball of string?' The important point is that you ask enough to illustrate his needs to him. Once you're in a position to do this it is important to commit him to the need and get his agreement by the use of 'tie-downs'. A tie-down is a phrase such as 'isn't it?', 'doesn't it?', 'won't you?', 'can't you?'. They are extremely useful phrases, as once the customer has agreed with you it is difficult for him to say no. If he does object later you can bring him back to this and remind him: 'As you've already agreed, Mr Smith, you wouldn't turn away from any extra business, would you?' or 'You said earlier that you need a new idea to help relieve the pressure of paperwork, isn't that right?'

A telesales person selling personalised Christmas cards could tackle it like this:

Telesales person:	'Would it be true to say that your company has expanded to a national market because of the quality products you offer?'
Prospect:	'Yes – and competitive prices. Word travels fast.'
Telesales person:	'At Christmas, Mr Jones, would you say good-will was more important or less?' (Here you are provoking the answer *more* – no one is going to say less.)
Prospect:	'More – we offer special Christmas discounts to our customers.'
Telesales person:	'That's a good idea for those customers who are prepared to buy at that time. What about your clients who don't buy in the winter?'
Prospect:	'Um, well, the offer's there.' (Now he's unsure – the telesales person must establish that need verbally.)
Telesales person:	'To maintain your image, especially during Christmas, you could do with something that extends your goodwill to all your customers, couldn't you?' (The sentence is ended with a question that demands a positive answer and leaves the path clear for you to tell the prospect about your product.)
Prospect:	'Yes, I suppose so.'
Telesales person:	'That's exactly why I'm ringing.'

The prospect has talked about his experiences, profitability and business attributes and implied that he needs to increase goodwill to all customers as a way of thanking them for their support.

How many questions do you feel are necessary at this stage? It may take one or two questions or more. It varies depending on the information you have been able to draw from your client. Consider an office

and business retailer as your prospect. You manufacture a new range of
filing cabinets which your current outlets are selling well:

Telesales person: 'How big a demand have you had for your filing
cabinets?'

Prospect: 'They go quite well.' (The salesperson now has
the opportunity to make him dissatisfied with the
present situation.)

Telesales person: 'So there is scope for improvement?'

Prospect: 'Yes.'

Telesales person: 'Our retail outlets DGR Evans and Co and
Brentinox, to name just two, have currently been
stocking our new slimline range of four-drawer
cabinets. They are selling as quickly as they are
given floor space. If they can sell them so
quickly there's no reason why you couldn't, is
there?' (Again ending the sentence with a
question. The need was established very
quickly and the product backed with a
testimonial – no prospect wants to be defeated
by his competition!)

It could take just one question:

Telesales person: 'How would you like to increase your stationery
sales by 10 per cent?'

Prospect: 'Who wouldn't?'

The salesperson then explains her company's plans to combine the
launch of their new range of quality stationery with various advertising
campaigns. All this will help to improve the retailer's sales as a stockist.

The sale

Desire

Despite being aware that one should 'never judge a book by its cover',
clients often do have preconceived ideas. Now, however, you are in a
position to present your client with a specific proposition. He will
listen now that you have committed him. The information pointer can

be more detailed here – learn it, so that your own personality is exposed, don't read it. Having established the need and restated it to ensure you have the right one, you can now offset it in favour of your product. Simply knowing your product is insufficient. People buy the same things for different reasons. Choose the right benefits and don't disguise them – you've got something to shout about. The more you tell, the more you sell, although how you sell is vital. Be selective and choose the right benefits.

The selling points and benefits for a van hire firm might look this:

Selling points	Benefits
1. Established for 100 years	1. Tried and tested (reputable)
2. All vans new and drivers experienced	2. Reliable and consistent
3. Open seven days a week	3. Convenient
4. 24-hour emergency service	4. Takes the pressure out of a crisis
5. Choice of size and type	5. Can hire/order what you need – therefore convenient
6. All vans for hire	6. Only use and pay when you need to – hire therefore economical
7. No deposit and invoiced on completion	7. Allows time to pay
8. Contracts available	8. Cost-effective
9. Unlimited mileage	9. Economical – only pay for hire time and distance no object

During charades, try linking the selling point with the benefit using words like 'which means'; for example: 'All the cars are regularly serviced, which means they are totally reliable, Mr Home'. The prospect can now listen. You must choose specific benefits, though, because no matter how good you prove your product to be, a customer won't buy unless you arouse his desires. Never give vague ideas; they won't help you sell either. People absorb concrete facts, not flowery allegories. They can become easily confused, especially over the phone where there is no visual contact. Select the important and appropriate benefits – the key benefits. By listing all the points in advance you can refer to them as you speak.

Unique selling points

A unique selling point or USP is extremely useful in the desire stage. It emphasises a quality that is reputed to be unique to you. Although it may *not* be unique, because you have highlighted it your prospect concludes that no one else offers this quality or benefit (including your competitors). For example, Marks and Spencer, who are renowned for their fresh chickens, labelled them 'Hand cut for extra leanness'. The Body Shop, selling skin care products among other things, said, 'All our products tested without cruelty to animals.' A dairy might say, 'All our milk is delivered in sterilised bottles.'

The implication is that the selling point is unique to you. Without too much thought you should be able to draw up your own organisation's USPs.

Testimonials

Now you are in a position to illustrate, by example, a success story of another client (if you haven't already done so earlier in the sale). Testimonials are one of the best sales tools you can have as they offer firm evidence in support of your claim. Collect a list and update it regularly – you will soon feel the benefits as stories of other satisfied customers will help to instil confidence in your prospect's mind. After all, if one of his competitors is successful because he uses you, then why shouldn't he be?

There are three simple rules to follow when using testimonials:

1. they need to be like for like;
2. they must be up to date; and
3. they must be credible.

If you don't have any information that is suitable, then use your organisation's good image as a whole to attain the prospect's approval.

Buying signals

A buying signal is an indication by the customer that he is keen to go ahead with the purchase, or at least interested. It may be obvious – he will exclaim his pleasure with expressions such as 'oh' or with actual commitments: 'that sounds good' – or it may be disguised and take the form of a question: 'What about the delivery?', 'How much is it?', 'Do you stock other lines too?', or a statement: 'I've heard you only sell by the roll', and so on. They can come at any stage in the sale and it is up to the telesales person to spot them. It would be far easier if you could catch his facial expressions or body mannerisms, but over the phone they have to be pinpointed through words and the manner in which they are relayed.

If a prospect is busy and is not interested, he would not waste his valuable time requesting additional information; he would try to terminate the call. Be positive. By remaining in control throughout the sale, taking his questions in your stride and acting on buying signals you won't lack sales!

A telesales person talking to a large agricultural company about a show stand, having established that the client is keen on attaining more clients, would proceed as follows:

Telesales person: 'Well, that's exactly why I am ringing, Mr Adams. As you know, our firm handles many successful trade fairs throughout the year. This year we are holding an agricultural fair at Witton Park in Cheshire, which as you know is a rural and extremely prosperous area. We have arranged for stands to be placed on the outer periphery of the allocated field so that the public, your potential clients, can circulate easily and not miss any of the companies participating, and the event will be held on the 6th, 7th and 8th of June when people are starting to get out and about again. We have run similar agricultural events in Herefordshire for the last four years and because of the enormous success we actually have a waiting list for this year's event. If the success rate is so good in Hereford, then there is no reason why it shouldn't be in Cheshire and I'm sure you don't want to miss out on your share of the market, do you, Mr Adams?'

Cost

Now we have reached the cost stage. Once you have a question on cost you can present it.

Prospect: 'Well no, but how much is it?'

If the question is not posed once the benefits have been given, you proceed naturally to this stage anyway. Many salespeople shy off when they come to presenting the cost. No matter how well you have stimulated the desire to buy and convinced the customer, it is a necessary part of the sale before you can conclude. To lessen the risk of a blunder, never presume that your quote is going to be unacceptable. You will have already established the size of the prospect's business, his overheads and market trends, etc, to help you ascertain the budget he will have to spend. Once you have calculated the possible size of the order you are free to quote. If the figure has been logically calculated it will be perfectly reasonable and you have every chance of its being accepted. Never be afraid of telling the customer how much; if you are wary, it will be detected in your voice and cast doubt in the prospect's mind – he will assume that your hesitation is because it is expensive for what it is. Remember, cost is relative! The cost needs to be cushioned and surrounded by benefits. By following the pattern of the sale, all the specific benefits you have used will have made your product sound a good proposition. You have already started cushioning the cost, so when you come to present it, it will appear minimal. Once the cost has been given, follow it up with a further benefit so that it has been completely sandwiched: 'On an order of ten you only pay £XXX per machine making an addition overall saving of £XXX on top of your usual mark-up price.' Or break it down, as in this example of a double glazing firm:

> Not only will you be saving money on heating bills, but for £XXXX you will have added soundproofing to warmer rooms. As the guarantee is for ten years, it works out at less than £XX per week, which makes it a real investment.

In both examples the emphasis is on what the customer gains. In the first, a straight £XXX; in the second, a completely double-glazed house for less than £XX a week. In effect you are shouting the benefits and whispering the cost.

Closes (action)

Once the cost has been presented, 'tie up' the order. Nothing is sold until you get that final commitment. Asking 'Do you want me to send them to you?' or 'Shall I go ahead and book that for you?' is inviting a negative response. Experienced salespeople know that despite a strong presentation, if the order isn't asked for properly it can result in a 'No'. Remember, when you have used a closing statement, give your client the time to answer and confirm that he has bought. Remain silent. The pressure is then on him to agree. If he disagrees then you have an objection to overcome (as illustrated in Chapter 6), otherwise it will be a 'Yes'.

To obtain that positive final commitment there are several types of closes you can choose from:

Alternative choice

As the name suggests, you give the customer an alternative. Whichever one he chooses he has bought: 'Is delivery more convenient for you on Tuesday or Thursday?'; 'Do you require the order in bulk or in lots of 10,000?'; 'Would you prefer a mahogany or oak finish?' Whichever you use, the customer has to make a positive decision.

Assuming acceptance

Assume throughout the sale that the prospect will buy. The final closing statement is a continuation of this: 'I'll have that sent to you next Thursday'; or 'Who shall we send the invoice to?'

Boomerang

The name gives the impression of something coming back. The close is used to confirm a client's wishes. By repeating a customer's question in a different way it can turn a buying signal into a firm order.

Prospect:	'Can I have a trade-in allowance?'
Telesales person:	'Do you want a trade-in allowance?'
Prospect:	'Yes.'

or

Prospect:	'Do you carry that line in green?'
Telesales person:	'If we did, would you buy it?'
Prospect:	'Yes.'

This close weeds out any misgivings or objections a client may have by turning his question into a positive commitment question. He will usually say yes, but if not, then at least you will know you have an objection in your hands which can be overcome.

Closes can come at any time: don't allow the moment to pass you by. The AIDA pattern can be used successfully, either applied rigidly or by missing stages. Provided the sequence is adhered to, the results will be the same. It's like a football match. The goal can be scored by the goalie at the other end of the pitch or by passing the various stages, or through a combination (see Figure 4.1).

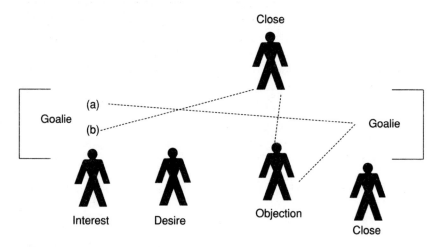

Figure 4.1   Reaching the close

A	**Telesales person:**	'Good morning, Mr Williams, my name is Mikki from Metal Supplies Ltd. We manufacture brass and copper items.'
	Prospect:	'I've heard about you. Tell me about your plant pots.'
I	**Telesales person:**	'Which sizes and designs tend to sell well for you?'
	Prospect:	'Generally medium – 15 cm diameter.'
	Telesales person:	'Why do you think that is?'
	Prospect:	'They are our most attractive range.'

Telesales person:	'So you are really looking for more appealing pots in a variety of sizes and patterns, is that right?'
Prospect:	'Yes.'

D **Telesales person:** 'We can help you provide your customers with a wider and more successful range. The brass range is particularly popular. It is an extremely durable range and has been lacquered to enhance the beauty of the metal, which means your customers won't have to polish them. David Basko Stores regularly order five dozen of each of our three sizes and Mr Basko says they all sell equally quickly. If he is attaining sales like that there is no reason why you couldn't, is there?'

Prospect: 'No. Is your delivery service still on Thursday?'

A **Telesales person:** 'Do you want delivery on Thursday?'

Prospect: 'Yes.'

The telesales person is now in a position to recap the order before completing the sale.

Telesales person: 'So that is five dozen of each of the small, medium and large brass plant pots to be delivered to Mr Williams at your High Street store on Thursday this week. Thank you, Mr Williams, and I will ring again in a fortnight.'

The telesales person has left the door open to return the call and possibly get more business – even a testimonial.

Closing the sale becomes instinctive with practice, like riding a bike. Remember, watch for buying signals and always get the customer to agree to order. Once achieved, confirm the details and *end the call*. Don't hang on and continue the conversation – it's not unheard of to talk yourself out of the sale again!

5 Telemarketing as a sales tool

Achieving good performance for most people is a journey, not a destination. Some things can't be sold over the phone and need a face-to-face approach. Telemarketing is becoming an increasingly popular area in business as a vehicle to gaining those face-to-face interviews. Indeed, 80 per cent of the top companies use it. Its potential has also started to be recognised by professionals as diverse as chemists, surveyors, solicitors and engineers as a route to developing networks in their field. Many of these professionals tackle the procedure themselves, and in so doing illustrate that to sell requires special qualities and not, as in their case, just qualifications. Once again, attitude is the key. You don't need technical experts to make the appointment, just good communicators. In fact, ignorance can be more advantageous than an in-depth knowledge in supporting your claim for a prospect's need to see an expert.

Making an appointment

In order to make an appointment over the phone you need to understand the AIDA techniques, so study Chapter 4 first. Although the decision is not a major one as you are not exactly selling your product, you are nevertheless selling the idea of a visit. You are instigating the idea that it would be worth your client's while spending a little time with you or a representative. Your prospect's time is valuable, however – time is money. The close is the booking of the appointment.

Your goal is to exude confidence and be believed. Clinch that favourable first impression by opening (and closing) your conversation on a positive note. Use the prospect's name – it shows respect and that you are speaking to him as an individual, not just another caller. I once worked with a girl called Julie Andrews – a great name for breaking the ice! – but one day she was put through to a prospect without being given his name. He picked up his receiver opening the call with his name 'Michael Jackson speaking' – you can imagine the rest!

Using a person's name is the best way to gain and keep attention. Successful communicators don't waffle but talk in short sentences and even in highlighted points. Almost everyone likes to be asked questions so don't be afraid to be the initiator. The prospect is, after all, in a position of authority, and to make important buying decisions he needs to be aware of what is available in the marketplace. Everyone in business has to keep abreast of the competition and is therefore more open to discussion.

The format is the same as 'cold calling' (Chapter 4). Introduce yourself, find out who you need to speak to and once you are connected use a strong opening to show why the prospect should want to see you. Give him a reason to make the appointment, ie a benefit that could arise from the meeting. After all, he has nothing to lose at this stage; he is only agreeing to a little time which could prove invaluable to him:

Start by using your information pointer – list questions you could ask, benefits, likely objections and answers, closes, etc (see Figure 2.2, page 14). Remember, those prospects are usually pressed for time, so that what you have to say needs to be concise.

Telesales person:	'Mr Witt, did you know that life insurance can cost as little as a few pounds a year?'
Prospect:	'Rubbish!'
Telesales person:	'Well, I was surprised too until I came to work here and the policies were explained. We could explain them to you, too – after all, a family's security is worth at least a few minutes of your time, isn't it?'
Prospect:	'What do you mean?'
Telesales person:	'Our representative will be calling in your area over the next few weeks. He will be able to answer any questions you may have and the visit is totally without obligation so you have nothing to lose but much to gain.'

Alternatively, you could be following up a mailshot:

Telesales person:	'Good morning, Mr Vaughan, my name is Gloria from Hayden Training; we've been in touch with your company recently. Can you tell me, do you use outside computer training?'
Prospect:	'Yes.' (If 'No', and you establish they are happy with their own facilities, then to continue with the call would be pointless.)
Telesales person:	'Who are you using at the moment?' (You need to know what you are up against – but remember: never knock your competition.)
Prospect:	'K & D Computers.'
Telesales person:	'Have you ever used any other supplier?'
Prospect:	'We are very happy with the service K & D offer and aren't looking for alternatives.'
Telesales person:	'I'm not suggesting that you swap, but it's obviously important to keep abreast of what's available in the marketplace. There may be occasions when you need support – perhaps a second provider, to help in unforeseen circumstances.'
Prospect:	'Possibly.'
Telesales person:	'We specialise in helping companies like your own and would like to make an appointment with you to highlight what's available so that as and when the need does arise you'd be able to get in touch with us.' (The prospect sees this as unthreatening and that it could be an advantage to learn more.)

Then close – ask for the appointment:

Telesales person:	'When would it be convenient for you, Mr Vaughan?'
Prospect:	'I'm free on Wednesdays.'
Telesales person:	'7 pm?'
Prospect:	'Fine.'

If he objects, ask for his reason, then answer it. Once you have over-come his reservations, ask for the appointment again. Don't hesitate or he will become indecisive.

You will have noticed the desire stage is virtually eliminated – the sale of the product/service is up to the person who will make the visit. Indeed, it can be an advantage to have limited product knowledge to validate your reasons for sending a colleague to visit. This makes telemarketing even faster than telesales but not quite as taxing. As with the actual full telesale, the technique needs to be carefully prepared and practised before the salesperson can succeed professionally.

A sample case

In Chapter 11 I have detailed more examples of scripts but for now imagine that you are making appointments for a more complex service and you're aiming to target blue chip companies in a very competitive field, eg incentive programmes. You need to prepare as many angles as possible, so your initial script, which will need rehearsing then paring down before you go on the phone, may go like this:

A: Good morning/afternoon, this is... from... I wonder if you can help me? Could you tell me...?

I: **Questioning techniques** (use past tense when necessary and select as appropriate):
● **Targets**
'Which time of year have you found most diffi-cult in terms of staff achieving targets?'
(If negative) 'Why do you think that is?'
(If positive) 'What kind of incentives have you run/been involved with? When do you expect to be the busiest time of year?'
● **Staff turnover**
'Why, in your opinion, is staff turnover usually higher in sales than in any other profession?'
or
'How difficult have you found staff recruitment on the sales personnel side?'

● **Incentives**

'How important is staff motivation in sales divisions and what effect does it have on sales?'

'What emphasis is placed on this?'

(If incentives are used)

'I'm very glad to hear that/it doesn't surprise me that a company like yours is tuned into the needs/expectations of sales people/staff. To arrive at the decision to use... I imagine a great deal of thought and planning went into this...'

(leads to yes).

(If incentives not used – use a testimonial.)

Establishing the need: 'Any way in which *(whatever you've identified)* could be improved upon would be of benefit, wouldn't it?'

'The key is undoubtedly staff satisfaction and reward. We at VRON Incentives have been helping firms like your own to keep abreast of the whole issue of staff motivation, targets and award...' *(to close).*

or

'I imagine that your firm is subject to constant change – to allow you to maximise on your own market – isn't that right?' 'In order to keep up to date in methods to help staff achieve targets...' *(to close).*

Close: 'I would like to take this opportunity to arrange for our representative/my colleague to visit you and discuss in more detail without obligation, your own specific requirements. When would be convenient to call?'

Objections (see more in Chapter 6): ● **Policy**

'Your market is subject to constant change and so are your staff. To keep abreast...'

(see establishing need and recap).

● **Budget planned**

'How far in advance do you plan? It is never too early to learn/see what's available, is it?'

● **Cost**

'The saying "speculate to accumulate" doesn't

apply here. Incentives/awards are paid on performance, aren't they? So the greater the performance the more profit the firm makes and the more likely staff are to achieve target – so there is no risk' *(use testimonial)*.

Objections, remember, are a plea for more information. The easiest method to overcome them is to remind the prospect of the need which you have already covered: 'you mentioned earlier/you said... was important'. But more of this in the following chapter.

Professionals

Successful communicators don't waffle – they talk in short sentences or even in highlighted points. The prospects you contact are in a position of authority. To make important buying decisions, they need knowledge of the competition and they are therefore more open to discussion.

Increasingly, professional establishments such as solicitors, architects and engineers are finding that they need to be more proactive. In other words, they need to make their businesses improve – they can no longer rely on the 'old boy' network and are having to bring new business into the practice themselves. These are highly trained individuals who are generally able to talk enthusiastically and eloquently about their work. However, in these professions there is often a huge psychological barrier that prevents them from bringing in business by using the phone. Indeed, the method is often perceived to be 'impossible' or at best 'unsavoury'. Breaking through the stigma is always more difficult. The problem is that we often think we know the right way to approach issues, but may actually be neglecting or avoiding the task in hand by clinging to established methods. It is all too easy to procrastinate, but by doing so these professionals are, in fact, avoiding the simplest route.

In the following scripts I have developed ideas to help professionals and other people arranging appointments on their behalf. Generally, the issues that block success can be dispensed with if you simply follow the format and the structure shown in the following examples. A point to bear in mind is that it can be an advantage to get a team member/assistant to make the appointments on your behalf. This technique can keep the conversation focused. If asked for detailed information, the assistant can say something like:

Assistant: 'I've been asked to help with the marketing and am not in a position to advise you on this. However, Mr Millward is an expert and he will be the person visiting. When would be convenient?'

Then you simply close the sale.

Let's look at these examples in fuller detail. Imagine you are a firm of civil engineers and you need to procure more work for the firm:

Telesales person: 'Hello, could you give me the name of the person responsible for procuring engineering projects?'

You may need to give a prompt: 'Sometimes it's the engineering manager, or it may be someone in operations or estates.'

Once you know the name, ask to be put through.

Telesales person: 'Hello, Mr Anderson, my name is Helen from the Peters Group. I understand you are the person responsible for engineering projects. Is that right?'
Prospect: 'Yes.'

If the answer is 'No', the contact will generally tell you who you need to speak to and you can asked to be transferred. You can also use this opportunity to ask for information so that you are better equipped when you do speak to the right person.

Telesales person: 'Are you familiar with us?'

If 'yes', move on; if 'no', just give a brief outline of your business. For example:

Telesales person: 'We are an international business consultancy with a background in engineering and the environment.'

Now you are in the *interest* stage – go straight in with a relevant point that relates to the industry and that highlights the negative issues and current drawbacks. You can incorporate it in the following way:

Telesales person: 'Because of [market pressure/a drop in share value/overseas competition], there is an increased pressure on us all to achieve improvements in productivity. It's widely recognized that resources are varied within organisations and are often limited.'

or

Telesales person: 'Recent government research has indicated that manufacturing will continue to expand its output, but with a labour-reduced force.'

Desire follows quickly – the sales pitch or presentation comes at the appointment, not on the phone. You are just whetting their appetite:

Telesales person: 'We are well used to providing specialist skills to enhance or support in-house projects.'

or

Telesales person: 'We ensure the best value for the project is achieved by examining both capital and running costs.'

or

Telesales person: 'We offer expertise with a fresh approach, and more and more sectors are beginning to follow suit.'

then

Telesales person:	'We are becoming increasingly involved with organisations like yours, whether by assisting in-house functions or carrying out entire projects, and basically we'd welcome the opportunity to come in and have a brief chat so that we can let you know more about us and, as and when the need arises, we'd hope you'd get back in touch with us. How is your diary looking over the next few weeks?'

If objections occur it's usually because the timing of the call isn't quite right and you need to establish when would be appropriate to call back. Make sure you do!

The success rate with an approach like this is usually good. The prospect needs to keep up to date and you will have demonstrated that you are not necessarily suggesting change, but an opportunity to review their current arrangements or dovetail with existing services when necessary.

Many professionals, once they have made an appointment, find that they are invited to tender for projects at later stages, which they might otherwise have only heard about through trade journals.

Another area to explore when trying to increase your client base is in 'partnering' – when one profession works alongside another. More partnering is occurring now than ever before – solicitors with accountants, accountants with IFAs (independent financial advisors), IFAs with solicitors, and so on. If you are doing this, think through your needs and the needs of your company. Compose a similar approach to that mentioned previously and keep it simple.

Take the example of an IFA partnering with a firm of solicitors. Once the telesales executive has established who handles personal injury/probate issues/joint pensions and divorce, etc, he or she can expect to speak to each partner in turn or arrange (via the practice manager) to make an appointment for a joint presentation either by inviting the solicitors to the IFA's offices or vice versa.

To demonstrate this, imagine that you are speaking to the partner who handles personal injury:

Telesales person:	'Hello, I'm Annette from Jones and Partners. We're independent financial advisors. Essen-

tially, with the increase in personal injury claims there is an increasing demand on solicitors to show due diligence and to help the client on to the next stage. You are no doubt aware that firms like yours often need the help of IFAs – especially when there is a larger claim and there may be a need to set up a trust. Many solicitors' firms are too small to draw on all areas of expertise from their own practice. At Jones and Partners we are becoming increasingly involved in helping by dovetailing our services and meeting this need. Essentially we'd welcome the opportunity to visit to briefly run over the services we provide and how these can benefit you. Then, as and when the need arises, we'd hope you'd get back in touch with us.'

Then *close* the sale as before.

An establishment providing a service to a broader range of clients (eg a bank) can use a similar approach, but can reinforce the need to arrange a visit with phrases like 'Obviously, we have a vested interest in your money being suitably placed/your hard-earned cash generating the maximum benefit/your banking requirements being the most appropriate for your needs at this moment in time.'

The key is to keep the approach simple and quick. Work with the AIDA pattern (see page 30). It is better to prepare too many questions, benefits, etc, because as soon as you have made one or two calls you'll naturally condense down your material and approach to suit the campaign in a way that suits you best.

6 *Overcoming objections*

Earlier we examined the importance of enthusiasm. It is the single most important component that a good salesperson can possess. All too often, however, you hear people saying that what they are selling is fantastic, and that it is the customer who is making a mistake by not buying it. This can never be true – there will always be a reason why a customer has chosen not to buy. It's your job to find out what it is and why.

The more experienced and fluent you become with handling AIDA techniques, the more experienced you will become at handling objections. Very few customers buy without reservations into the proposals you have put forward. In driving a car there are many factors to consider on your journey – pedestrians, other vehicles, weather conditions, etc. In choosing to buy, a prospect similarly has a range of considerations and it's your job to tease them out. The secret behind handling and overcoming objections successfully is to remain calm and professional but not allow yourself to be drawn into an argument. If you do, then *you* will lose, not the customer.

People usually object because they are unsure that what you are offering is really going to satisfy their demand or fulfil their need. Very often this is because they have misunderstood you and are seeking more information. If you interpret objections in this way and remain positive and show a degree of empathy, the prospect is then aware that you are able to appreciate his reservation. Your answer will ultimately be more welcomed by him. Objections can occur at any stage and be about any aspect of the sale; for example:

- 'It's a quiet time of year.'

- 'I don't sell upmarket products.'
- 'I am happy with my current supplier.'
- 'It's too risky.'
- 'It's too expensive.'
- 'Don't give me the sales pitch, I've heard it all before.'
- 'I'm not interested.'
- 'Ring me in a few months.'
- 'I don't need it.'
- 'I don't like your products.'

The list is endless. You should write down the most common ones you experience. By doing so, you will be able to pinpoint the major objections to your products and act on the answers accordingly.

Often a prospect will object simply to try to throw the salesperson off the track, perhaps unaware that he is throwing in a red herring – a defence mechanism against being sold anything. More often though, it is a disguised plea for more information. If the prospect was genuinely uninterested he would simply say, 'No thank you' and hang up. It is the task of the salesperson to isolate the objection to find out whether it is a true and valid one or not. It is a waste of time answering every obstacle posed because you end up sounding petty and argumentative. To concentrate on discovering what the trouble really is, you need to ask:

- 'Suppose that were not the case, would you go ahead?'
- 'Assuming you had proof that this can save time, would you buy?'
- 'Apart from that you'd go ahead?'

For example, imagine you sold ink to printing firms and the customer says, 'I'm not sure.'

Telesales person: 'Assuming you had convincing evidence that the ink is as good as I have said, then would you order it?'

or

'You need reassuring, don't you?'

If the answer is yes, then the telesales person goes on to give the customer a testimonial. This is where the '*Feel–Felt–Found*' approach comes into its own. Quite simply, you say that you 'understand his feelings, indeed others have felt this way and (that) in your experience you have found... works'. If the answer is no, then the customer usually comes up with another objection which changes the context:

Prospect: 'Not exactly, I think it's very pricey.'

Now she has a cost objection. To see if this is the true objection she continues:

Telesales person: 'So apart from the cost you'd go ahead with the order?'
Prospect: 'Yes.'

The telesales person can now strive to overcome the cost objection with confidence that this is the prospect's main concern. With cost objections too much empathy can be a disadvantage – don't dwell on it by giving reasons for the price increases, competitors' price increases forcing yours up, etc, as it ends up sounding like an excuse or apology. You need to establish how pricey it is in the prospect's view, and to do this you can ask him directly: 'How much is too much?' or 'What are you currently paying for...?' or 'What did you envisage the price would be?'

Telesales person: 'So you are currently paying £X per gallon less for your ink?'
Prospect: 'Yes.'

Now you need a testimonial:

Telesales person: 'Are you familiar with Printolike?'
Prospect: 'Yes.'
Telesales person: 'They have been using our ink for the last three months and have found its quality not only gives their product a far more professional image, but that their higher prices to cover the costs have been readily accepted by their clients because they are so impressed with the results. If they can achieve impetus like that, there is no reason why you couldn't, is there?'

Because the true objection was isolated and forced into the open, it enabled the telesales person to use a testimonial which in turn increased the prospect's confidence and made him more aware of the importance of image and quality.

Another way to handle a cost objection is to find out how much is too much and break it down until it becomes minimal:

Prospect:	'It costs too much.'
Telesales person:	'How much were you expecting to pay for the plastic sheeting?'
Prospect:	'About £200 per roll.'
Telesales person:	'So we are talking about a difference of £20 per roll?'
Prospect:	'Yes.'
Telesales person:	'You said earlier that you make, on average, 500 bags out of each roll, Mr Jones. That would work out at just an extra 4p per bag and the quality of the sheeting is so superior that you can print your client's logos on without affecting the density of the design.'
Prospect:	'Um.'
Telesales person:	'If you wish to buy our cheaper range we can of course supply you, but you would not be getting the same value for money or, of course, the same quality.'

The telesales person has used comparable products in the sales range and distinguished between 'cheaper' and 'more value for money'. Customers usually decide to buy items of good value rather than lower-priced onces.

Another way of tracking down the genuine objections is to seek a better understanding of the client's views by quite simply asking 'Why?'

Telesales person:	'You obviously feel very strongly about not using our company, Mr Smith. Can you tell me why you feel that way?'

Because you have acknowledged the prospect's feelings and shown a willingness to understand, the prospect will usually respond. Once he does, you will, by listening, be able to establish what his real reservations are and overcome them accordingly.

The new business you are seeking through cold canvassing will undoubtedly be sought by your competitors. The prospect may already be committed to another firm or at least be considering using them. Your product knowledge and knowledge of your competition is valuable here. Never discredit your own firm by knocking your competition; better to gain a smaller order or be used as a back-up supplier where you have a chance to build a client's confidence. If you handle this account well, eventually you could become the sole supplier. Think of future orders, not just the present targets. Accept gracefully and assure him that he will not be disappointed – rather than telling him how wise he would be to change. Your discretion will be respected as you gradually gain his confidence.

Objections on regular accounts

Sometimes objections are not so obvious. Rather than stating the problems a client may start reducing his orders or change supplier completely. This indicates dissatisfaction. We know prevention is better than cure. If you suspect a client has a problem – perhaps he is more reserved or suddenly impatient or cool when you've normally had a good relationship – start delving by asking directly what is wrong: 'Are you completely satisfied with us, Mr Yates?' or if you suspect he has a specific grievance: 'Are you happy with our delivery times, Mr Strong?' Once you have found the problem you then have a tangible objection on your hands, which is much easier to handle.

Equally, a prospect whom you may have contacted four or five times and with whom you have built up a certain rapport may still not have given you an order. Stop beating around the bush. If you know he needs the products or likes the idea, ask 'This is the fourth time I've phoned you, Mr Johnson, at your invitation and each time you say you are very interested and yet you haven't ordered; be frank with me – do you need me to call?' The client is placed in an awkward situation. Your annoyance is justified, that is obvious. It is true, he did ask you to phone back each time but never got round to preparing an order. He is likely now to reassure you and do something positive by placing an order. Even if he had not bought, you could have made a firm future date. There may be a genuine reason – perhaps he is not opening his new shop for another six months because of labouring difficulties. If so, then you obviously can't expect to sell now. Better to build a relationship on the information by acknowledging the problems and arranging to phone back when it is time.

Indecision

'I'll have to think about it'

Recognising a buying signal is a prerequisite to a successful call. Occasionally a prospect will wish to mull the idea over in his head before making a firm commitment: 'I'll think it over.' You have presented the sale and found a real need. It is imperative that the sale is closed. If the decision to buy is postponed, when the telesales person phoned back, the mood to buy that has been created in the desire stage will have worn off and the prospect will no longer be eager. Acknowledge his thoughts – he is indicating that he is interested or why would he even think about it? Ask him what he has to think about or why. By helping the customer analyse his own thoughts you can often tempt the main objection through:

Telesales person: 'Obviously we'd like to do business with you. I can appreciate that you would like to think it over, it indicates to me that you're interested. Just to make sure I've explained everything properly, would you tell me which particular aspect you would like to think about?'

Then go through the sale and points again, leaving the cost until last:

Telesales person: 'Is it the time of year?'
Prospect: 'No.'
Telesales person: 'Is it the hours?'
Prospect: 'No.'
Telesales person: 'Is it the quality?'
Prospect: 'No.'
Telesales person: 'Then is it the cost?'
Prospect: 'Well, it is rather a lot.'
(You now have a firm objection to overcome.)

Telesales person: 'I fully understand your reservations. Obviously the capital outlay is considerable, but the wrong cleaning contractors could add £8,000 to your annual expenses, whereas the right one could save you £3,000 per annum. Our service is especially suitable because...'

You then go on to relay the important benefits and attempt to close the sale again.

To illustrate the handling of this objection showing the whole sale, imagine you are selling a special motoring feature in a local paper that circulates just outside your prospect's area. The advertisements will be appearing in late July:

Telesales person: 'Mr Edwards, I wonder if you could give me some information, please? I noticed your advertisement in the *Gazette* last week and wondered, do you get most of your business from the local area or further afield?'

Prospect: 'Mostly local, but a few travel from surrounding towns.'

Telesales person: 'When has been the busiest time of year for the sale of new cars?'

Prospect: 'August for the new registration, then January.'

Telesales person: 'So if I could show you a way of capitalising upon the very buoyant new car market at this time, you'd be interested, wouldn't you?'

Prospect: 'Yes.'

Telesales person: 'Well, I can do just that for you through our highly successful annual new registration feature in our *Express* paper called "New Registration Extravaganza". It has a full banner heading which will look very striking on the page. All the ads are uniform size to complement the appearance and a reader competition is included. Just think, Mr Edwards, only £XXX for a guaranteed readership feature because to enter the competition all the ads have to be read. The prize is twenty-five gallons of petrol, which is a big incentive, isn't it?'

Prospect:	'It's too expensive.'
Telesales person:	'How many cars would you need to sell to make a profit?'
Prospect:	'One.'
Telesales person:	'So if I could get that customer you'd be interested, wouldn't you?'
Prospect:	'Yes. But I'd like to think about it.' *(A red herring – you know it's a cost objection.)*
Telesales person:	'Fine. I'm glad you're going to think about it because obviously you are interested, aren't you?'
Prospect:	'Yes.' *(The barrier is down now – the prospect thinks he's off the hook.)*
Telesales person:	'By the way, before you go, is there anything you're not clear about? Is it our papers?'
Prospect:	'No.'
Telesales person:	'The time of year?'
Prospect:	'No.'
Telesales person:	'Then is it the cost?'
Prospect:	'Yes.'
Telesales person:	'Well, assuming cost was not a factor, then you'd go in the feature, wouldn't you?'
Prospect:	'Yes.'
Telesales person:	'Are you familiar with Smith's Garages, Mr Edwards?' *(He's Mr Edwards' main local competitor.)*
Prospect:	'Of course.'
Telesales person:	'Well, I spoke to Mr Smith himself and he said that he sold four cars through this feature last year and you're not going to turn away the sale of four new cars, are you?'
Prospect:	'No, of course not.'
Telesales person:	'So would you like to promote your estate cars or your sports range?'
Prospect:	'Well, can I put something in about my used car sales?'
Telesales person:	'Would you like to promote them too?'
Prospect:	'Yes.'
Telesales person:	'Right. I'll have the artwork drawn up similar to that in the *Gazette* while you draft the copy and

	I'll ring you back on Thursday after lunch... shall we say 2.30 pm?'
Prospect:	'Fine.'
Telesales person:	'Thank you, Mr Edwards, goodbye.'
Prospect:	'Goodbye.'

Wait for the client to replace the receiver first – if you don't, it will appear rude and as if once you've got what you want, you've run out of time for him. It's a small but very important point, so do it.

Conversely, if you are a supplier with a variety of items to sell and you discover by using this technique that the client, having said he will think it over, has no need of the things you mentioned, ask, 'How can we help you, then?' You may discover he needs another part of your range which you neglected to mention, or perhaps your competition has offered free delivery and he would buy from you except for that. If you can arrange what he requires, then do so, but don't make any promises you can't keep – when you say you can do something be absolutely sure that it will be done.

'I'll speak to my partner'

It should have been established at the beginning of the sale that the prospect is not the sole decision maker, so you could have arranged to speak to each decision maker separately before they got together to discuss it, or perhaps arranged for a representative to call. If the partner is new to you, don't allow him to speak to his partner first, if you can avoid it. As with the secretary, the story will be second-hand when it is referred to and although he will have a vested interest, his information will not be as convincing as yours:

Telesales person:	'Who is your partner, Mr Samuels?'
Prospect:	'Mr Armstrong.'
Telesales person:	'Perhaps I could speak to him first. I know how busy you are and he may ask a question that you are unable to answer or seek further information.'

This doesn't always work, of course, but it's worth a try. If he insists on handling it himself, then confirm that he's keen and that it all rests on his convincing his partner.

Telesales person:	'I see, so can I take it that if your partner agrees with you, then you'll go ahead?'
Prospect:	'Yes.'
Telesales person:	'Then I'll leave it in your capable hands.'

He is less likely to come back with a negative response as that would be an admission that his partner has more 'say so'. If he says 'no' then you can ask him what his reservations are by going through the points again as in the 'I'll have to think about it' example to isolate the true objection.

Cancellations

Although cancellations do not happen regularly, they are not uncommon. On occasion a client will, after you call, have reservations and doubts about his decision. Because his views start conflicting, he seeks to eliminate the decision causing the dilemma. This means cancelling. When he cancels, try to find out why. You may be able to overcome the problem areas. It isn't easy though; it is safer to watch out for feelings of doubt and any reservations during the call. If the customer appears hesitant when he orders, he is probably lacking in conviction and this will lead to cancellation. To avoid this, reassure him by giving him your phone number and asking him to call if any problems arise. Follow up your call with any extra information to see the order is followed through, eg check specific times of delivery to his firm if possible.

Send him any further information or illustrations of the product that you may have to support your claim. If you learn of a suitable reference or testimonial later, phone him back and tell him about it. All this helps to confirm in his mind that his decision was the right one.

If cancellations happen regularly, check your technique. You could be overkeen and appear bombastic and overpowering. The client, feeling intimidated, could then order because he feels forced into submission. After the call and having gathered new strength he may then cancel.

Train your non-sales staff

Any member of staff who has dealings with the public in a potentially selling-orientated situation should be fully equipped in AIDA – especially handling objections.

For instance, a car service engineer who is fitting tyres for a client who has left the car with him for a few hours could receive a phone call to check that the vehicle is ready. It could be that the engineer has found that there are further faults that are virtually undetectable to the non-expert and will need to sell the idea accordingly.

Engineer:	'Your tyres have been prematurely worn by the shock absorbers, which need replacing.'
Prospect:	'I haven't noticed anything wrong with the car.'
Engineer:	'No, you wouldn't – you see, the shock absorbers wear very gradually. As they help maintain the right wheel balance and tracking and help to protect many aspects of the control and safety of the car they make a very important contribution to braking, steering and cornering. The problem is that because they wear very gradually most people subconsciously adjust their driving to compensate for this wear.'
Prospect:	'I'll think about it for next time.'
Engineer:	'It would be false economy to delay the replacement, Mr George, because, as I have already mentioned, the damage they could cause to other parts of the car could mean even more replacement parts next time. As for your own safety and that of your family – I'm sure you wouldn't put a price on that, would you?'
Prospect:	'I see what you mean.'
Engineer:	'We have the shock absorbers in stock, Mr George. I could start the replacement now and your car will be ready for collection by 5 pm this evening. Will you be calling in then or would you prefer to leave the car overnight?'
Prospect:	'No, I'll collect it at 5 pm.'
Engineer:	'Fine, I'll make sure everything is ready. Goodbye, Mr George.'

Any objections become more easily handled with experience and practice. Always welcome them. They are certainly not an obstacle as they represent an opportunity for you to reassure your clients.

7 *Setting up your own telesales unit*

Having become experienced in telesales, you are now ready to set up a telesales room and controls. If your telesales unit is to succeed, a great deal of thought and initial preparation are required. The best telesales team in the world will fail if the apparatus and back-up systems are not correct. Before setting up a unit you must detail what you will need as a minimum requirement, examine your budget versus the costs you will entail and finally scrutinise your market carefully. This chapter will help you in your initial planning.

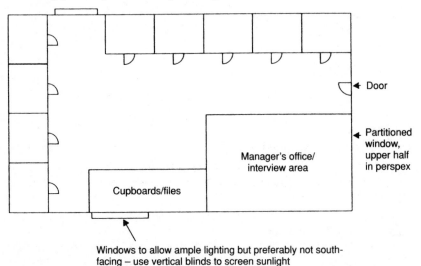

Figure 7.1   Telesales room layout

Apparatus

Obviously, call centres will have the facilities and technology installed at the outset (see Chapter 8). You would expect this with a large or multinational organisation. However, smaller firms and those just starting up will need to build up gradually.

First and foremost you will need office space and equipment – obvious items like desks, chairs, filing cabinets, etc. The work of the telesales staff will be intensive – healthy atmosphere can be created in the most unlikely office environments provided there is suitable basic equipment. You may wish to use existing furniture, which is perfectly acceptable if it is strong and there are enough files to cope with the extra paperwork (telesales units can so easily become cluttered as the throughput increases in spite of IT installations. Perhaps you could look at Information Management Software). The most practical way to lay out a telesales room is to put desks against the walls (see Figure 7.1).

Ensure there is adequate light – preferably an office allowing natural daylight through; if not, the lighting must be strong enough for staff to carry out their paperwork without straining their eyes. On the other hand, if the light is too bright it can cause a glare from the paperwork which results in all types of problems, including migraines. Sit yourself in the office you propose to use for a day or two and test its feasibility first.

The desks should be partitioned off by using sidescreen perspex clipped to the desk and up to about three feet above the desk top, allowing staff to see one another. While giving privacy and relative quiet it eliminates isolation. Desks should have ample drawer space and shelves for disclosures, order forms, etc. Everything should be at the telesales person's fingertips (see Figure 7.2).

Your most expensive initial outlay will probably be the telephone system you have installed. It is also the most important piece of equipment. The size of your unit and the requirements of the department will predetermine your phone system to a large degree but they should include the following:

- **Headsets**
  Headsets should have one earpiece only. Headsets allow for free movement of both hands, which is important, especially if using a computer/word processor. Equally, if you have to search for an

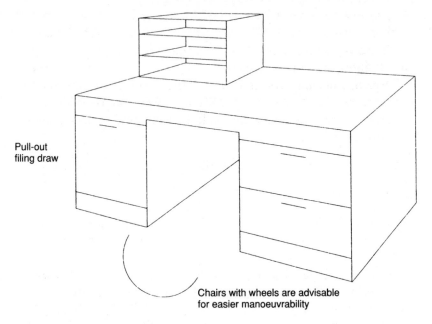

Shelving above the desk for directories, order forms –
alternatively, use stacking baskets. Leave ample room for PC.

Pull-out
filing draw

Chairs with wheels are advisable
for easier manoeuvrability

Figure 7.2 Telesales office desk

item while talking to clients you usually end up trying to balance
a manual set between your chin and shoulder – this requires
some concentration and it will detract from the call itself. I stress
one earpiece because I have heard many people complain that if
both ears are covered it can cause headaches as the sound is too
condensed and unnatural.

- **Monitoring attachment**
  Ongoing training is a prerequisite to a successful telesales unit.
  Your telephone system should make allowances so that when
  you have recruited staff you or your manager/trainer are able to
  sit with the telesales person and monitor the call without being
  overheard on the line – no echoes whatsoever. This will be a vital
  training aid, so make sure you are entirely happy with any
  system you look at before making your decision.

- **Sound control**
  The volume of the bells on the phones should be controllable so
  that you can reduce the sound to suit the department. If you

anticipate a larger unit it is worth considering a light indicator to replace the bell, which can be a noisy distraction.

● **Manual receiver**

A manual receiver is not essential but useful for someone to use if passing a ringing phone and wishing to take the call.

● **Queuing system**

Again, a queuing system is not essential, but if you anticipate a large number of incoming calls it is worth considering as it allows callers to be dealt with in turn, thus reducing their frustration.

It is important to check the current rates per unit for making calls so that you can anticipate your next phone bill.

These are a few ideas to help you make the right decision. If you look through your local telephone directory under 'telecommunications equipment', you could arrange for an expert to visit you and establish just what your requirements are.

Soundproofing is also important. The noise and buzz created in a telesales unit can become unbearable for both the telesales person and the client. Soundproofing can be ensured either by using proper screening or by attaching perspex to the desks – your local office equipment outlet should be able to advise you.

Correct equipment is necessary to ensure better results and so too is stationery. Consider your product, the systems you currently use – will they adapt or be suitable for a telesales unit? How will information be stored? Who needs to be informed? How will communication filter through to other departments (eg dispatch, accounts, etc)? Does the sales team have the facility to check back?

Computers can seem inflexible when you are talking to someone and are dictated to regarding the order in which you must extract information. However, if properly used, and provided you keep the customer in the picture, the overall process is speeded up and efficiency is improved. Technology is so advanced now that it would be appropriate to seek professional advice on the best systems to suit your own business needs.

Using an agency

If you decide to seek outside assistance in setting up your unit there are a number of agencies that can help. First, unless you know of an agency or profession that can help, you should phone your local Business Link, who will know if there are any local businesses that can help with telesales. Obviously it is up to you to assess their suitability before you commit yourself. Find out what experience they have in this field, and after telling them what your requirements are, ask how they can help. If you are satisfied then you may proceed. Costs can vary enormously depending on how long you require the agency's service and for which aspects of selling. You may be looking for someone to set up the whole unit from the outset to include direction on apparatus, stationery, recruitment, training and implementation, or simply to give you advice and provide you with a structured format and a stage-by-stage list of areas to cover. There are many grants available to assist companies with training and you may be eligible. Simply phone your local Business Link, who will be able to help.

Assuming the agency you have chosen agrees to carry out the project, then you will be ready to draw up a contract, which will be legally binding and cover all the aspects (including rates) that you have agreed.

A typical agreement would follow the pattern shown in Figure 7.3.

Fred Bloggs & Co

This Agreement has been prepared to ensure that, from the commencement of the Company *(Fred Bloggs & Co)* and consultancy *(X Y Training)* relationship, both parties fully understand their respective rights, duties and procedures.

This Agreement is made between *X Y Training ('The Consultant')* of (address) and *Fred Bloggs & Co* (address) for work as a consultant in connection with:

The *Consultant* and *Fred Bloggs & Co* have agreed to the provision of consultancy services on the following terms:

1. This agreement for the services of the *Consultant* covers the period of XXX to XXX. Consultancy services will be provided for X hours per day and for X days per week. No payment will be made during periods of absence which occur for whatever reason unless agreed by *Fred Bloggs & Co.*

2. The consultancy fee will be XXX per day, and a car mileage allowance of XX pence per mile which shall be invoiced on a monthly basis covering the dates worked during that period and scheduling in detail the aspect covered and mileage incurred.

3. The fee is to cover work associated with:
   (list areas to be covered by consultant)
4. The *Consultant* will co-operate fully with *Fred Bloggs & Co* and take the initiative in offering advice and services. *Fred Bloggs & Co* agree to assist the *Consultant* in the performance of these duties by making available to the *Consultant* all relevant information.
5. The *Consultant* shall not, without the permission of *Fred Bloggs & Co*, disclose to any person outside the Company any information obtained during, or in connection with, his/her consultancy with *Fred Bloggs & Co.*
6. This agreement may be terminated at any time after an initial period of XXX by either party giving not less than XXX written notice of termination to the order.

Dated ....
Signed by the Consultant   Signed by Fred Bloggs & Co

Figure 7.3   A typical agreement

Use the guideline and adapt it to suit your own requirements.

Essentials

Earlier in the book I made reference to the legal changes that affect companies that use the telephone to do business. Although the continuing growth of the industry can be attributed to an increase in consumer demand, ie offering the personal contact and service that consumers have come to expect, a proportion of consumers still do not welcome telephone offers. These laws are designed largely to protect private individuals, sole proprietors and partnerships from receiving unsolicited calls (but do not currently apply to larger organisations). Your prospects may have opted for inclusion on a telephone preferencing service (TPS) list. These lists are updated monthly and it is your task to check whether your prospects are in them.

In addition, the Data Protection Act (DPA) is now in force, governing client confidentiality and associated rules. The office of the Data Protection Commissioner is based in Wilmslow and can be contacted by telephoning 01625 545700 or visiting the Web site www.dataprotection.gov.uk.

It seems logical that you would consider buying validated marketing lists if these rules apply to you. Indeed, if you have any specific target requirements, this method can help identify leads for you. Your local information library can help, or you can check in the *Yellow Pages* under 'direct mail'.

A London-based company provides a service in all three areas and to all types of business sectors. It is a trade association called Direct Marketing Association UK (DMA), and can be contacted by telephoning 020 7321 2525. It is a very useful resource if you need advice on how to go about generating external leads.

Do make sure that you are covered and operating withint the realms of the law, as hefty fines can be enforced if you are not.

8

Get organised! Administration of the telesales unit

We live in a world where records and achievements are constantly improving. Telephone selling is fast, and for any sales operation to be successful, effective administration procedures must be implemented to enable the best possible result to be achieved. Record cards and filing systems need to be kept as simple as possible. Programs can be designed to incorporate specific data to suit your company needs. Call centres use many sales resources. It is an all-embracing term covering telemarketing, sales, service, reservations and operations. It is a generic term but in essence is used by firms that have a large team of telephone operatives who will need specific resources to suit. The likelihood is that they will use more sophisticated telephone switchboards or dialling systems to support their campaign. These are called ACDs (automatic call distributors). Telesales people work in a rapidly moving market. To help keep the atmosphere free from undue pressure they should have vital information at their fingertips. Installing the right software is imperative. You will need the following records – adapt them to suit. Many contact management programs are appropriate – they allow faster access and eliminate the need to make mental calculations.

If, however, you do have ACD installed, many of the following systems will be inappropriate, as the system can be linked to your computer and will generate leads, diary dates, phone numbers –

whatever you require. The following section can be recorded techno-logically. The system will also feed information to managers on how staff are doing, how long calls take, how effective they are, etc. This helps to identify training areas. However, assuming that you need to function on a provisional manual level, the following is appropriate.

Record cards

Record cards are vital for enabling this information to be collated – salespeople are very important market indicators. They are in direct contact with customers and prospects. Each day your staff should fill in a daily record sheet that will allow them to carry information forward for future reference onto the record cards. Daily record sheets will also enable them to go back to no reply or engaged calls later in the day. No matter how good a memory your staff may have, if they are absent for any reason would another colleague be able to step into their shoes easily?

Daily forms

Daily forms used in conjunction with a diary help enormously. The headings can vary to suit your own requirements (see Figure 8.1).

The heading 'Number of calls' will help you monitor each person's total input. The easiest method of recording calls which I have used is to treat each digit as a dial spin. The line ╱ is a bar on which to rest each digit, eg ⑊, which equals three calls as each digit represents the telephone number for that client having been dialled. It may take several attempts to get through and speak to the person in authority to buy as the phone may be engaged or the receptionist may ask you to call back. Once you get through to the decision maker the call becomes an effective one – demonstrated by the cross: ✕ , showing three attempts to get through and a fourth successful one. If a sale is achieved then it becomes a productive call, illustrated by a circle: ⊗ The bottom of the daily form is for totals. This part can be completed by a clerk or a telesales person at the end of the day. This provides an invaluable source of information for your own records and stock control; the recording of performance and allocating bonus and checking against targets.

Daily Form Name: Jane Jonson							
Date	Contact	Time	Order	Postdata	Call back	Comments	Number of calls
21 April	J. Williams	9.15	–		Next month	Off sick	
	BAR	9.30	10 × a		2 weeks	Another order	
	Jakeo Ltd	9.50	–		2 months	Negotiating new sites possibly interested in cables	
	Ansaspeke	10.05			2 p.m.	In meeting	
	J. Bloggs	10.10	8 × b		Next week		
Volume sold	Revenue sold	Stock sold			Effective calls	Productive calls	Total
18	£200	A – 10 B – 8			3	2	6

Figure 8.1   Daily form

Daily call rate forms

The columns should then be transferred to separate sheets showing weekly and monthly figures. Ultimately you will be able to make direct comparisons with the previous year, which will help you with future forecasts (see Figure 8.2).

Master forms

Once the figures for the month have been logged they can then be transferred to a master form (see Figure 8.3).

The following abbreviations can be used on the master form:

- LY – Last Year
- TY – This Year
- E   – Effective
- P   – Productive
- T   – Total

Daily call rate Name:		Effective	Productive	Total calls	Comments
w/c 4/1/88	Mon	15	10	20	½ day hols
	Tues	25	16	38	
	Wed	30	20	39	
	Thurs	40	32	50	
	Fri	19	13	28	
	Total	129	91	175	
w/c	Mon				
	Tues				
	Wed				
	Thurs				
	Fri				
	Total				

Figure 8.2 Daily call rate form

Call rate: 87/88 Daily average	January		February		March		April		May	
	LY	TY	LY	TY	LY	TY	LY	TY	LY	TY
Name	E P T	E P T	E P T	E P T	E P T	E P T	E P T	E P T	E P T	E P T
Jane Jones										
Sue Brooks										
Joanne Bill										

Figure 8.3 Master form

Sales staff may change their role during the year and move to a different area. If the room is split into territories which makes it easier for some people to ring more clients than others, because of the specific products they are selling, you may prefer to compare last year's territory with this year's to give a better picture. If you tried to compare the telesales people's figures they would give a false reading.

Bonus forms

The daily form totals also register sales and volume. This information could be transferred to a bonus form ready to work out the payments at the end of the month (see Figure 8.4).

Stock records

Finally, the amount of stock sold needs to be recorded in order to keep tighter controls on ordering. Again you may wish to keep last year's figures to make percentage comparisons of buying trends for the next order – do sales increase in the spring and if so, by what percentage? You can then, on a pro rata basis, assess your ordering requirements for that period (see Figures 8.5 and 8.6).

Name		Month	
Territory			
Target: £6,000			
		£	
w/c 4/1/88	Mon	350	
	Tues	280	
	Wed	150	
	Thurs		
	Fri		
w/c 11/1/88	Mon		
	Tues		
Total:			
Average:			Bonus paid £

Figure 8.4   Bonus form

Weekly stock record

Month: March   Week commencing

Name	Product A					Product B					Product C					Product D					Product E				
	M	T	W	T	F	M	T	W	T	F	M	T	W	T	F	M	T	W	T	F	M	T	W	T	F
Jane	1	3	4	6	2																				
Sue	4	6	1	–	1																				
Joanne	1	1	8	2	3																				
Weekly totals	6	10	13	8	6																				
Grand weekly totals	43																								

Figure 8.5   Weekly stock record

Month: March

	Product A	Product B	Product C	Product D	Product E
Current stock	300				
Week 1	40				
Week 2	62				
Week 3	48				
Week 4	84				
Monthly total	234				
Current stock	66				
To order	At this stage you can look at the buying trends over the previous years to determine your percentage increase or decrease in orders.				

Figure 8.6   Monthly stock record

Mastercards

Once an order has been placed, the information can be transferred to a master account card (see Figure 8.7). You need one for each client. Any future dates for non-regular clients can then be keyed in under the relevant date in the diary. Not only do record cards indicate the account potential but comments can relay vital information about the market.

Name:

Address:

Type of business:

Name of contact:

Relevant details:

Call – Once/month

Orders:	Week	Amount	Comments
	1	6	
	4	6	
	6	12	

Figure 8.7 Mastercard

Order forms

Order forms (Figure 8.8) need to be straightforward and designed to hold all the necessary information to allow orders to be processed. They should include date, name, address, order, price quoted, ordered by whom, quantities or order, delivery dates and invoice number. Several copies of order forms are required, so self-carbonating forms are preferable if you are not on computer. It is advisable to use different-coloured sheets for each department to eliminate confusion. One copy is needed for invoicing, one for initiating dispatch, one for stock control and recording and one for your own files.

Leads

The telesales office needs to be structured in such a way that each salesperson knows what the others are doing. Leads should be split either alphabetically or geographically or into type of business. This will help canvassers avoid overlapping their calls. Occasionally a new client will be contacted by more than one person. If this happens, apologise and then ask tactfully what he decided to do. A different voice at a different time of the day could result in a previously obnoxious prospect changing into an amiable client. Any new accounts you achieve should, along with existing accounts, be contacted regularly.

	Date:
Name:	Tel No:
	Ordered by:
Address:	Order No:

Order/product: Quantity: Cost:

Total price:

Delivery date:

___

Special details:

Salesperson:

Figure 8.8   Order form

This is called servicing the account. It helps you to keep on top of orders and builds good customer relations as your efficiency increases.

As far as possible, ensure the order is followed through. The quality of your firm's service will be reflected in the amount of care your telesales personnel show their clients. It is the client's means of measuring the depth of professionalism, which can only serve to enhance the image you will have already created.

In call centres, where high-volume sales are handled, the ACD can have system filters to deliver phone numbers and connect you to that number quickly, effectively fact-finding for you. The rate at which we have progressed and continue to progress with the help of technology is astonishing. However, do remember that this is a 'people to people' job – no matter how sophisticated the technology is, the right people with the right attitude and training are imperative.

9 Recruiting telesales staff: who and what to look for

Once you have set up the telesales unit and are satisfied with the systems and controls, you will be in a position to start planning the staffing side. First consider the size of the unit and decide how many staff you will require and indeed can accommodate.

Telesales staff will expect to receive a basic salary plus unlimited bonuses. Perhaps you would prefer to test the telesales unit's success before employing any significant number of staff. If you can afford to recruit a minimum of two staff then do – it is important that telesales personnel have immediate competition and someone to discuss calls/clients with. If this is not possible, try to make sure someone else will be in the office to act as support.

Staff turnover may, at times, seem abnormally high, when in reality people generally move for domestic or career reasons. The former are out of our control, while to an extent the latter are preventable. Salespeople, especially telesales personnel, work in a fast-moving and constantly changing environment. After around eighteen months to two years of selling, a successful person generally seeks a greater challenge – either a promotion within the organisation or a move. Unfortunately it is not always possible to promote, and invariably you can expect a telesales person to seek a more demanding role elsewhere or you risk the possibility of their being headhunted. If this is the case, then being in sales ourselves, we should look upon it positively and see it as a compliment. If you recruit wisely and train your staff well, it is only natural that they should yearn for and achieve progression. It would certainly be more worrying if staff turnover at this level were non-existent. People can become stale.

With regard to the scarcity of good salespeople, it can often be an advantage to recruit a totally inexperienced person who has little or no knowledge of selling. If the interviewee's character and personality are suitable then the fact that they are 'raw' is irrelevant – people completely new to sales are often easier to train. They are more open, flexible and adaptable to your training techniques as they have no preconceived ideas or direct comparisons to make.

But what are the basic ingredients for a good telesales person? You have probably been asked by people outside sales how on earth you cope with your pressurised work. What they don't realise is that the environment is largely up to the individual. A good telesales person will be somebody with confidence, a desire to do well, someone who shows signs of self-motivation through enthusiasm and ideas – a person who is keen to learn and prepared to take on a challenge. Very often, successful salespeople are those who are highly motivated and possess the characteristic of having clear personal goals which they seek to achieve through their performance. People without goals, who cannot identify their aims, are usually less willing to make an effort. A few searching questions at the interview will reveal this very quickly. People who do not know what they want out of a career, what they expect from a job or why they really applied in the first place (some people do actually give that impression) are obviously not going to be suitable.

We all know the saying 'A bad workman blames his tools.' One of the reasons for the phone's questionable reputation rests here. The flaw lies not so much with the phone as with the operator.

Why should this be? Why is it that when the growth in business is so apparent the key workers are so neglected?

This neglect isn't just prevalent in training. To understand how the telephone can work against you, you need to address a stage even further back and question your staff selection.

You wouldn't, for example, ask a receptionist at a busy doctor's surgery to help reduce waiting time by seeing a few patients herself. Although it is true to say that specific qualifications are unnecessary in this type of work and businesses often utilise their existing resources, the job of telesales does require a specific type of personality.

A successful telesales person is going to need to stretch her communication skills to the limit, for there are no visual prompts (body language normally counts for 55 per cent of the strength of a message). She will also need to be confident, have a desire to do well, show signs of being self-motivated through her enthusiasm and ideas; in short, be someone who is prepared to learn and prepared to take on a challenge.

A potential telesales person needs to show all the positive qualities and more. I have already mentioned an eighteen-month to two-year time span for working at a particular role. At the interview stage you will need to ask yourself a number of questions about the interviewee. Does she show promise for the future? Will she be able to plan, organise and lead others? Executive qualities can be spotted at interview occasionally, even if they are just a glimmer – someone who has sound ideas on and ambitions for life itself and talks with authority and conviction about her experiences could, with good training, be nurtured.

Remember, too, that good salespeople are often difficult to handle because of their outgoing characteristics. Obviously professionalism is vital, but there is no point in employing someone who is going to be deliberately awkward. Similarly, a placid person is equally unsuitable. A person who is a little extrovert but shows signs of willingness and helpfulness is usually a safe bet. If she is presentable, communicates easily and above all sounds cheerful and you feel she would fit into your sales environment, then follow your feelings. Remember, too, that as your telesales people cannot be seen by your clients a clear voice is extremely important (see Chapter 1).

Advertising for telesales staff

To attract the right kind of staff you may decide to advertise the position in your local paper. Correct staffing will be crucial to the success of your unit. If you have the time to train staff intensively you may be looking for someone with limited or no experience whom you can 'mould' to your work of working. Alternatively, you may be looking for someone who has been or is currently involved in sales and has at least an insight into what is required, even if the pattern does need remodelling. Either way, you will be trying to entice a certain type of person to apply for the post. You will need someone strong and self-motivated who has the ability to converse with people at all levels. Someone who is outgoing and confident; who has a clear voice and is able to relay information (or answer your questions at interview) in a concise manner. Telesales staff are usually ambitious, outgoing people who will welcome a challenge provided they can reap the rewards (a good bonus potential and prospects). All this needs to be relayed in your advertisement. It must be designed in such a way that it will attract the right people to apply. While most newspaper staff will advise you on the wording of your advertisement and the areas you should cover, it is sensible to have an idea in mind, such as that shown in Figure 9.1.

It is advisable to ask applicants to phone in the first instance – even if it is just to tell them to write in enclosing a full curriculum vitae. The voice is so important that if someone sounds totally unsuitable, then no matter how good their CV is, you shouldn't even consider an interview.

TELESALES

required

- Bored with your current work?
- Looking for a challenging new career with prospects?
- Are you articulate and numerate and educated to GCSE standard?

If you can answer yes to all three then we would be interested to hear from you.

Due to expansion within our organisation we are currently seeking telesales staff to work five days a week 9.00 am to 5.30 pm. Experience is not essential as full training will be given. The work will be demanding but extremely rewarding with a real opportunity for those looking for a career with prospects. Good communication skills are a prerequisite for this post and the applicant will need to show flair in handling people. The vacancy offers a good basic salary and excellent bonus potential together with real opportunity for promotion within a busy but happy working environment.

If you think you could stand the pace and have the qualities we seek, phone Jane Clark on 020 …

Figure 9.1 Example recruitment ad

The interview stage

Once you have arranged the interview times, ensure that the office is ready to accommodate the interviewees and that no one will interrupt you. Allowing for the fact that all interviewees will be nervous, your interviews should follow this simple structure:

1. Make the interviewee welcome. Introduce yourself and any other colleagues who may be present (there shouldn't be more than two of you to one candidate – you don't want to intimidate them!). Allow them time to sit down comfortably, possibly making casual enquiries about how they travelled to meet you and if they had any difficulty in finding your offices – this helps to relax the person.

2. Explain the format of the interview – that it will be an informal chat where both parties have the opportunity to find out a little more about each other and that if there are any questions, you will allow time for them at the end. Then tell them how soon you are likely to be able to let them know.

3. Tell them to relax, and throw the ball into their court by asking them to tell you a little about themselves, eg what they enjoy doing in their spare time, etc. This serves two functions: it acts as an icebreaker, allowing time for the interviewee to drop the barriers, and it allows you to make an initial assessment.

4. Next ask about their schooling/career to date (if lengthy, just the more recent details). Ask about a typical day in their current job – duties, etc and, most importantly, what they like and dislike about it. This will allow you to assess the similarities to the job you are offering and how any experiences will relate to and aid them in their new role, if successful. Ask what the current employer would say about them if you phoned for a reference (look out for timekeeping, reliability, etc).

5. Find out what enticed them to apply for the post you advertised and what they think the job entails (anyone who has done their homework will give a reasonable answer to this – again aiding your decision).

6. Once their perception of the role is established, enlighten them. Explain a little about the company, its origins, products and future ambitions; also about their role and how it would fit into

the masterplan. Include working conditions, holidays, pay, prospects, etc.

7. When they have heard a little about the job, ask what qualities they think you are looking for in telesales people and why you should choose them. This prompts a real opportunity for would-be successful staff to sell themselves. You may also ask them to do a brief charade, eg 'Sell this pen to me.' At least if someone is attempting to answer your questions and remains fairly confident they are more likely to be successful.

Some additional probing questions might be:
- 'What motivates you?'
- 'What are your good and bad points?'
- 'What type of personality do you think we require?'
- 'How would you handle an aggressive customer?'

8. Finally, ask if there are any questions they would like to ask. They *should* have prepared some.

This brings the interview to a natural close. Explain that you have other candidates to see and then you will either be drawing up a shortlist for second interviews or be making your decision. Let them know when you expect to be in touch and how (letter or phone). Ask whom you should contact for references – some salespeople are good at selling but hopeless at securing jobs for a variety of reasons. Check *all* references: you don't want a disruptive influence in your company. Thank the interviewee for attending and see them out.

Usually you can form an opinion by following this structure. If you wish colleagues to be involved, arrange for second interviews.

Job description

Although you will have given a brief description of the work at the interview when you have appointed your staff, ask inductees what they perceive their role to be and how they see their position in the hierarchy of the company. Very often they see themselves as staff at the bottom of the ladder whose role is to answer the phone (sometimes experienced telesales personnel will express similar thoughts – this shows signs of demotivation). It is crucial that they realise just how important they are. Telesales people are extremely important and valued members of any organisation. They are the people responsible for handling your customer's enquiries, orders and even complaints. As far as your clients or potential clients are concerned, they are the company, and first impressions count. It does no harm to remind telesales personnel of their importance; it not only boosts their confidence, but makes them more receptive to training, which in turn helps to keep them on top.

The emphasis on the role of a telesales person is to sell. They are salespeople who, having realised their importance and understood the role, will be eager to receive assistance in selling skills. Training is vital to help analyse weaknesses and improve strengths. A receptive frame of mind is therefore a prerequisite to a successful learning session. How to set about training is detailed in Chapter 10. Until then the book concentrates on vital topics.

Attitude

Selling is extremely pressurised work. Targets need to be met and we expect more and more from our staff. Because of the nature of the work and the kind of staff you employ, keeping them informed helps to keep them motivated. People need to understand why their jobs exist, so by reminding them of their importance within the company and training them in sales techniques, you are, in turn, showing how they contribute towards the desired results of the organisation. Staff need continuous training to keep on top and avoid bad habits. One of the golden rules when handling telesales people is to explain why they are being trained in particular areas and why it is so important to get it right. They soon learn that the company is investing time and money in them, not to be critical, but to help.

Psychology

One of the key factors to remember when training telesales people is not to overtrain. In their eagerness to use the correct techniques they can sound 'brainwashed' and unnatural. Our potential clients cannot see our sales staff and they will rely on their expertise and professionalism. However, our competitors are equally well equipped, so why should our clients buy from us? It is important to stress that while applying the techniques and retraining their mental attitude and approach in sales, telesales people must maintain their own personalities. People warm to individualism as much as honesty and integrity. In selling we encourage staff to maximise on all selling opportunities but we need to create and maintain the goodwill of the prospect. Think for a moment of yourself window shopping. A sales assistant approaches you, you talk, then you return home happy and tell your family that you have bought a special present for a friend whose birthday is next month. You were not looking for a present on this occasion, and yet you bought. You don't say that the shop assistant sold the item to you – if you did, you would have been acutely aware of sales pressure. You bought it. This is one of the keys to successful selling – remember, nobody likes to admit to being sold anything, but they are persuaded to buy! Ensure your staff are aware that customers will buy provided they understand their needs and know how to persuade them.

Positivity

The power of persuasion has to start somewhere. Your staff should recognise first what a customer is generally looking for: value for money, reliability, credibility, professionalism and efficiency. A tall order indeed – so what kind of attitude should your salespeople have? Quite simply a positive one. Positive phraseology is vital. Anyone talking on their own subject sounds positive because they have the knowledge. This in turn makes the delivery confident and we accept it. Think of a solicitor or doctor. You turn to them for advice; they may ask a few questions and then draw a conclusion or plan of action. In selling, your staff should draw information from clients to ascertain their need of the product in just the same way. They should start by retraining their attitude. They should stop using negative phrases like 'I think', 'Perhaps', 'Maybe', 'Do you want?', 'Presume', and so on, and think positively – 'Others have found', 'You need', 'Look at it like this', 'We deliver on...', 'To help you now', and so on. The effect on the prospect is also positive as your staff will have allowed themselves to project their professionalism, their confidence and their enthusiasm and the client will listen.

The results of the sale are equally effective – by taking the initiative in the conversation your staff will have gained control. They will encounter fewer difficulties because the prospect will rely on the advice of a professional person.

In contrast, your staff being negative can have adverse effects, as seen in the following poem:

Think Big
(Source unknown)

If you think you are beaten, you are,
If you think you dare not, you daren't,
If you'd like to win, but you think you can't,
It's almost a cinch you won't,
If you think you'll lose, you're lost
For out in the world you'll find
Success begins with a fellow's will –
It's all in the state of the mind.

Full many a race is lost
Ere ever a step is run,
And many a coward fails
Ere ever his work's begun.
Think big and your deeds will grow,
Think small and you'll fall behind,
Think that you can and you will,
It's all in the state of the mind.

If you think you're outclassed, you are,
You've got to think high to rise.
You've got to be sure of yourself, before
You can ever win a prize.
Life's battles don't always go
To the stronger or faster man,
But soon or late the man who wins
Is the fellow who thinks he can.

Anon

Teach your staff that as the brain controls the body, being negative or pessimistic can promote fatigue, apathy and unhappiness. Optimism or positivism promotes a feeling of vitality, happiness and the ability to get out and get cracking.

Induction of new recruits

Knowing and appreciating the success of telephone selling will help your staff to understand why this market is growing so rapidly. They must, however, understand the disadvantages so that they are able to avoid the pitfalls.

Disadvantages

No visual contact

Telephone selling still has an image problem, particularly with calls to people's homes. Fortunately, as expertise grows on the salesperson's part, this is diminishing.

Young children often give their interpretation of a story or idea in a fashion that makes us smile. A child once told his mother that his friend did not go to bed because there could not be any beds in his house as there were no stairs. The child was quite right – there were not any stairs. The friend lived in a bungalow, but because this three-year-old had no experience of bungalows, he determined that it was a house without bedrooms. If you look at this example in more depth and relate it to adults – more specifically to clients – how often do they have preconceived ideas of what a product or service can do? Their knowledge may be extremely limited, but this does not prevent them drawing conclusions. As prospective clients cannot see a telesales person or the product, then their image is not confirmed or corrected visually.

Limited capacity to listen

Opposite are ten simple questions. Read them out to your staff, asking them not to compare answers but to write down the answers that first enter their heads. Explain that it is not an intelligence test but a fun exercise with a purpose that will become clear at the end. Read each question only once, and stress that you expect them to be honest with their marking.

Questions	Answers
1. Do they have a fifth of November in America?	Yes
2. Some months have 30 days, some have 31; how many have 28 days?	All do
3. If you had only one match and entered a dark room where there was an oil lamp, oil heater and some kindling wood – which would you light first?	The match
4. If a doctor gave you three pills and told you to take one every half-hour, how long would they last?	One hour – you would take one on the hour, one at half-past the hour and one on the hour
5. A farmer has 17 sheep; all but 9 die. How many does he have left?	Nine
6. A man builds a house with four sides, each having a southern exposure. A big bear comes wandering by; what colour is the bear?	White (it must be the north pole)
7. Divide 30 by half and add 10. What is the answer?	70 – many will have 25 as they have divided 30 by 2
8. Take two apples from three apples. What do you have?	Two apples
9. How many animals of each species did Moses take on the Ark?	None. It was Noah!
10. If you drove a bus with 42 people on it from London, stopped at Watford to pick up 7 passengers and drop off 5 more, and at Luton you dropped off 8 and picked up 4 and arrived at Edinburgh 20 hours later, what was the driver's name?	Your own name (the question starts 'If you...')

By now your staff should be in uproar! Go through the answers and remind them to mark fairly. On average people get under four right. Very few get over six. The purpose of the exercise is to show your staff that because they rely only on voice and words over the phone, they must be extremely careful about what they say. Usually only up to 85 per cent of what is said over the phone is taken in. The results of the test obviously exaggerate the point; nevertheless the point will have been made and taken in.

Those are the two main disadvantages. Now that your staff are aware of the problems they can set about avoiding them.

Advantages

Now that you have created a light-hearted atmosphere you can ask your staff to think of the advantages of telephone selling. Use a spider chart to illustrate this – you can then put down the answers as they are given (see Figure 9.2).

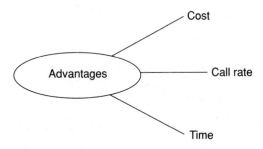

Figure 9.2   Spider chart

Add your own prepared examples if necessary. The information given should include:

- cost;
- call rate;
- time and convenience;
- speed;
- flexibility;
- use of word pointers;
- assistance from colleagues;
- no visual distraction;
- one-to-one sales;
- making appointments.

Finally, the most important benefit is that the telephone takes priority –
if people are queuing to buy tickets and the phone rings, the last two
tickets could be sold to the caller on the phone, the people at the front
of the queue having to go without.

This method of illustration shows your staff quite clearly that the
advantages more than outweigh the disadvantages – staff can see just
how lucrative it is and understand just why they are so important. As
telesales personnel learn how to avoid and cope with the problem
areas, they begin to recognise the assets, which in turn all helps with
motivation. The more they know and understand, the more confident
and proficient they become. There are no geographical hurdles to overcome, and minimal frustration when the client is engaged or out of the
office. Telephone selling is fast, efficient and direct.

10 On or off the job? The importance of good staff training

A great phenomenon of life is that from the moment we are born through to our last breath we are always learning. We start by grasping fundamentals, motor skills, language, etc, then we receive education – facts and information walking hand in hand with our own experiences in life and our parental direction; until finally we mature and recognise that expertise and know-how are something that is ongoing.

But how do we learn? Psychologists say there are four main areas through which we acquire our knowledge:

1. our own experiences;
2. observation;
3. concepts and generalisations;
4. activity.

To expand on this, think of a car showroom. You want to buy a car but you have no idea what type, colour, size, etc. To make your decision you will use all four learning concepts:

● **Experiences:**
You look at the car, touch it, sit inside and realise that it has certain gadgets.
● **Observation:**
The salesperson tells you about the car, where the indicators are.

- **Concepts and generalisations:**
  Next, for example, you are told that the car does 50 miles to the gallon – information that leads you to recognise that it is an economical car to drive.
- **Activity:**
  Finally, you test-drive the car and feel for yourself its comforts, performance, etc.

Sales training should allow staff to learn in all four areas, and it too should be ongoing. We are never in a position to say, 'I know it all'. How many times have you been on a one-day course and come away enthusiastic and vowing to put everything you've learned into action? And how many times have you found yourself slipping back into the same old routine as soon as you get back into the office? Staff need training regularly to be kept motivated and competent at their work, which means a more profitably run organisation achieved by a willing and motivated team. We live in a world of constant change and it is crucial that we allow our employees the chance to develop and mature while acquiring sales wisdom.

This chapter, then, is devoted to all aspects of training.

Whose role?

The role of a trainer is an extremely important one. Training is vital. While sales staff are usually self-motivated individuals, they will need guidance and direction from someone they can look up to, trust and respect – even experienced staff can slip (they can become complacent and switch to 'automatic pilot', for example). The keys to success are good communication skills and the vision to look broadly at the task in hand. Take driving as an analogy: with a great deal of experience you can find yourself driving home or to work without really registering the route – let's face it, we become 'dangerous drivers' not giving due attention!

In sales, complacency is equally dangerous. No two calls are the same. We must stay alert to face the constant challenges different prospects/clients present. As with any profession, selling needs to be worked at, not taken for granted. The need to keep fresh is vital.

A trainer is a manager who will have to plan and organise the department, set and achieve objectives and ensure that the staff are motivated by communicating with, training and developing them. She will also need to evaluate their performance by recognising strengths and weaknesses of individuals so that she can iron out those weaknesses and maximise their strengths.

This is a very responsible and demanding role. To reach those requirements you, as a trainer, will need managerial qualities and more. Probably the most important prerequisite is that you yourself can sell. If you can't, how can you possibly command the respect of your staff? You must also be reliable – showing good attendance and punctuality – because you will be leading by example. You have to strike a happy balance of trust between yourself and the sales team and your duties as a manager and reaching objectives.

If you decide to recruit a trainer, the person you will be looking for is someone who can command authority and respect with dignity and who is seen to be, and is, genuinely concerned with the welfare of the staff and the smooth running of the department. Someone who can empathise with people and their traumas in life and who can instil confidence and guide someone in their goal to become salesperson of the year!

It is not an easy role. Often, people who are both 'trainer material' and show potential as a manager cannot achieve this balance. They feel that they would become too far removed from their friends and be seen as a traitor! This all sounds unrealistic, but if a trainer cannot detach herself from her 'pals' then you won't get the true picture – yet if she detaches herself completely, the staff won't go to her for help and advice.

What is training?

Training is teaching – imparting information successfully so that individual sales staff develop the sales techniques required in a smooth but fast-running department.

There are three main ways in which you can train:

1. 'On' the job, where you are sitting with an individual while she is working on the telephone.
2. Monitoring at random, where you have the facility to listen in to any call from your own office phone.

3. 'Off' the job, where you take your team into a classroom situation allowing for group teaching and discussion.

All three are important in their own right, so let us examine each area in depth.

On-the-job training

Here you have the chance to coach your staff on an individual basis. You do not want to be seen as a critic, someone who is looking for weak spots; but as a person who can help individuals improve their performance. Just as selling entails a great deal of psychology, so too does training.

To be able to impart your information and guidance to maximum effect you will need to know your individual staff well. Explain at the interview and on induction courses that training is ongoing and the reasons for it, so that it doesn't come as a great shock to the employee when you first sit with them.

Individuals' needs vary enormously. Sales techniques need to be practised regularly. Good salesmanship depends on three factors:

1. **Knowledge:** Product knowledge, knowledge of your market, of the customer and the competition.
2. **Belief in one's product:** Show your staff how successful the company is, how it has grown and how your clients have benefited from buying from you.
3. **Persuasiveness:** The ability to persuade people to buy.

To help your staff become good salespeople you should sit with them regularly – at least four hours a week depending on their needs and those of others. If you are sitting with a telesales person for the first time, you obviously won't know what their sales weaknesses are. Ask them how they are getting on and get them to show you how they are organising their work and following administrative procedures. Good trainers, by asking a few open questions, should encourage elaborate answers. Because the sales staff will be doing most of the talking, you will see how they react to different areas of their work and, more importantly, you are taking the pressure off them – they won't be seeing you as someone who is checking on everything. Simply start by asking them to take you through a typical call and the administration procedure. Ask them what they think of it and how they feel. Trainers should be open to ideas – encourage staff to think of ways of improving the system; it not only gives them the chance to help you but, more importantly, makes them think about what they are doing and why.

Once you have talked a new person through the procedure, ask if you can listen to a few calls. They are unlikely to say no – if they do, you can simply ask why and assure them that others, including yourself, had that reaction when a trainer first sat with them. In time we all grow to realise that a trainer only wants to help.

Before you start listening to a call, make sure you have a pad of paper and a pen with you. Don't rely on your memory. Write down the conversation as applicable – picking out points not only that you could improve upon, but things that were good and you can praise. A trainer's golden rule when analysing calls should be praise, criticism, praise – 'cushioning' the weak areas, just as a salesperson cushions the cost.

Imagine your salesperson followed the AIDA pattern of a sale until the prospect objected. She is angry because the presentation was good and the objection, in her view, was unreasonable and she lost the sale. Follow this procedure:

- Ask why she felt she lost the sale. Most experienced telesales people will usually tell you what went wrong and what they should have said, but somebody who is new will need to be coaxed.
- Ask how they could have rectified the problem. This serves two purposes – it allows the telesales person to think of an alternative and it enables you, as the trainer, to assess their ability at problem solving in sales.
- Suggest you both go through the call again together – this is where the notes you have taken are invaluable. Go through the call step by step. Don't try to train on every single point, it will overpower your trainee, but select one or two major points. First *praise* her. Even if the call was atrocious – perhaps her voice was nice and clear, so tell her! Look at the problem area and ask if she can think of an alternative, if she can. Then suggest one yourself. Once you have illustrated the point, go on to another strength and end the note on praise.
- Look at another prospect and charade the call with her first, ie get her to practise the call on you first while you pretend to be

the prospect. Cover the same ground and see if her responses have changed in the sale.

- Briefly discuss the charade, then get her to make the call. It should be greatly improved and mirror the training you have just given.
- Assess and praise the call. Even if it was unsuccessful but had improved, say so. Be generous with your praise but be *very* careful not to overdo it because you will lull her into a false sense of security.

Occasionally a telesales person will make a diabolical call but will achieve her aim and get the order. If this happens, what do you do? Believe it or not, absolutely nothing. If you try to train a girl who has just been successful she won't believe you. Why should she? The AIDA pattern is internationally proven as the most successful sales format. People who wander from it but remain successful are few and far between, so if the success of the call was a fluke you will have the opportunity to train on those weak areas again.

To train *on* the job successfully you need a quick mind. No two calls will be the same, so your reactions must be those of an accomplished salesperson. In your eagerness to help it can be difficult to isolate the important areas to train, but as with selling itself, you will develop a good training technique with practice. Remember to empathise with your staff and watch carefully for their reactions to your suggestions to see whether your approach is working.

Once you have established a training pattern, go over the past session and let her know each time you sit with her what you will be looking for. Experienced salespeople should be able to recognise their own weaknesses and after each call tell you where they went wrong and why. It is still important for you to add alternatives. It is surprising how many different answers to the same objection you can give.

Apart from actually listening in on calls and charading, on-the-job training can be used to look at administrative procedures, checking attitude and helping to learn a little more about your staff. Obviously you don't want to spend the whole time socialising, but it is a 'people' job and it is far too easy to lose sight of that in your eagerness to impart knowledge.

Eventually you will reach a stage where your staff should come to you, totally unscheduled, and tell you about a call they have just made – whether they couldn't overcome a certain objection and are seeking your opinion or even allowing you to share in the satisfaction that a good successful call brings. When this happens you will reap the rewards of a good trainer. Your staff have recognised your ability and your concern for them and because they trust you and rely on your opinion they will be able to approach you at any time.

Monitoring at random

This type of assessment is useful for establishing what type of training is needed and whether or not the sales staff have understood and are using the techniques they have been taught. It is not essential to have telephone equipment that enables you to do this because although it is useful, you can sit with individuals anyway. However, sales staff are less likely to slip back into bad habits because they know that you have this facility. If you do hear a good call, let them know. Similarly, you must discuss errors.

If a pattern emerges among staff, monitoring will give you a good indication of group training areas for the classroom situation.

Off-the-job training

This form of training is invaluable. It enables you to cover areas in which there is a general training need but also gives staff the opportunity to talk about and share their experiences and to bounce ideas off each other. Training in a classroom situation requires a great deal of planning. You will be dealing with staff with varying degrees of experience and while you don't want to bore the experienced, you don't want to neglect the newer members. You will need plenty of ideas to make the sessions interesting – we will cover this later.

Off-the-job training should take place each week. Decide when your quietest time is and set aside one hour for the session when the staff will have the opportunity to be taken completely away from the job and allowed to develop and learn in a different environment.

Decide on the topic for your session and plan how you are going to deliver it. The session should enhance performance and prompt revision. Use cue cards to highlight the important areas you wish to elaborate on. These can be small postcard-size cards that are discreet and easily referred to. They should contain one-word pointers that will prompt you – just as the salesperson uses a guideline script, so too will you in training. The structure of the sessions should remain the same although the topics will obviously change.

Your cue cards should follow these lines in a condensed form:

- **Welcome.**
- **Introduce to session:** Try to think of a new approach to an old session. For example, if you want to train on openings you could ask them to imagine they are at a dance with a girlfriend and they are approached by a man who wants to get to know them. Ask them to think about what type of approach he would have to make to get them to respond, then go round the room to find out what they say. There should be a variety of very different examples.
- **Relate the introduction to the session:** We all require different approaches to encourage a response. The same applies to our clients. You wouldn't use a familiar opening on a new prospect, for example. Explain that the aim of the session is to look at the different openings in different situations and analyse their successes.
- **Ask questions:** Set the scene; for example, a newspaper article shows that a bicycle shop is changing premises and they are selling shop fittings – ask how they would open the sale. Asking leading questions is vital in off-the-job training; information they contain will stimulate a response. The bulk of the work should be done by the staff. They have to think of an answer, give it and say why they have made that decision. To ask questions successfully don't leave them open for anyone to respond. If you do, you will find only the experienced staff will answer. To encourage everyone's attention you should use the three Ps – **p**ose the question, **p**ause while you look around then **p**ounce by naming a person to answer; for example, 'What type of opening would you use in XY situation *(pause)* Alison?' You will have the full attention of the whole class because they won't know who you are directing the question at, so they will all be thinking of an answer. Always recognise their efforts in an answer; for example, 'Yes, you could ask that way; does anyone else have another idea *(pause)* Jane?' Never say 'that's wrong' but encourage participation. It will be obvious which the best answer is without demotivating anyone and discouraging their future involvement for fear of ridicule.

- **Chart the answers on the board:** Make sure all the openings are covered.
- **Summarise the session.**

So the cue card should look something like Figure 10.1.

Openings	
Welcome	
Introduction:	meeting a new person at a party
Questions on openings:	using 3Ps ■ Knowledge ■ Observation ■ Complimentary remarks
Chart:	answers
Summarise	

Figure 10.1   Example cue card

You may need to use several cue cards for each session. Because they are durable they will keep for future sessions – you could start your own training index.

Off-the-job sessions should be light-hearted and encourage staff to participate. Ensure you give equal attention to all members – eye contact is especially important but don't stare! Make everyone feel that their contribution is welcome.

Finally, end the session by going back to the objective and tie it up by getting the staff's mutual agreement that the aims (ie looking at alternative openings in given situations) have been met. This confirms not only that they recognise the importance of this type of training but that they have indeed learned or revised this area.

What type of training – how and when?

Training can be used for a variety of reasons, from ironing out specific difficulties to introducing new ideas. Preparation is obviously important. You wouldn't ask a novice in horseriding to demonstrate jumping skills to an advanced group – the pressure would be too great and would provoke failure, which in turn would demotivate the rider. For exactly the same reasons you need to prepare carefully the type of sales training session you are going to use and to what extent you want individuals to participate. New members of the team will benefit from the mere presence of your experienced staff initially, while the remainder can be actively encouraged to demonstrate their expertise and revise and develop their skills.

There are a variety of ways in which you can use group training sessions to stimulate all your staff, some of which are noted here.

Quizzes

These can be given individually or better still in a 'knock-out' form; for example, split your team into two groups, ensuring you have an equal mix of experienced and inexperienced staff. Give each group the same list of questions and toss a coin to see who starts. Explain that the leader of the starting team (Team A) selects a question and asks the named person from the opposing team (Team B) to answer, but they must know the answer themselves. If the question is successfully answered then Team B gets two points; if not, the member of the other team (A) may answer and gain one point. But if they fail to answer they lose a penalty point. Once a score has been allocated then the person to whom the first question was directed (Team B) selects another question to ask a member of Team A, and so on. This promotes competitiveness and gives you the opportunity to see how your staff react in a team effort – it will also help you assess sales weaknesses and leadership qualities in individuals.

The following list of questions can be used for a general exercise or you could draw up a list of specific sales examples within your own company.

1. Give an example of a 'boomerang close'.
2. Answer the objection 'it costs too much'.
3. What type of opening would you use on a regular client?'
4. How would you handle a late delivery complaint?
5. What is a tie-down?
6. What is a leading question? Give an example.
7. Give an example of a unique selling point.
8. What is a benefit?

9. What are the rules when using a 'complimentary' opening?
10. What is a testimonial?
11. How can you isolate a 'true objection'?
12. At what stage in the sale should you remain silent?
13. What are the rules for handling an aggressive customer?
14. Give an example of a buying signal.
15. Give an example of overcoming the objection 'I'll think about it'.
16. What is the mnemonic that sums up the pattern of a sale? What does it stand for?
17. What is a committal?
18. Why should questions be posed in the past tense? Give an example.
19. What is the task of the salesperson?
20. How should you treat an objection?

All the answers have been covered in this book. Although the questions are very general they serve to give you an idea of how to organise a quiz.

Challenge

Another variation in off-the-job training is to strive to prove that if one person is determined enough, persistent enough, persuasive enough, etc then they can have a tremendous influence on other people. The exercise is called *Getting priorities right* – a survival exercise for which you will need two teams or more with at least three to four people per team.

You will need to prepare two handouts for the exercise, as follows:

Getting priorities right – a matter of judgement

Imagine you are sailing in the tropics when your boat is shipwrecked. The boat is going to be destroyed completely, but you have five minutes to decide what items you can take with you to a fortunately nearby desert island. You will arrive on the island wearing only the clothes you stand up in and with your eight items safe and sound and in working order. However, you cannot just take any eight items – you have to take 8 from the choice of 12, in order of priority.

Following this you will work with your group and produce a group list – again in order of priority. You will need to appoint a chairperson who will be able to defend the team's selection at the end of the exercise. The team exercise will last approximately 59 minutes and then we shall lead a discussion and assessment of the results of each group together.

Suggestions:

You need to show your reasons for choosing each item and its position on the list. For example, would the alcohol be used to drink, or as an anaesthetic or disinfectant? Would you need a penknife or would you rely on the first aid box containing scissors?

List of items   **Own order**
   1. Watch   1.
   2. Bucket (enamel)   2.
   3. Penknife   3.
   4. Compass   4.
   5. Spade   5.
   6. Bottle of brandy   6.
   7. First aid box   7.
   8. Ball of string   8.
   9. Magnifying glass
  10. A Bible
  11. Box of pencils
  12. Telescope

Team order   **Reason**
   1.
   2.
   3.
   4.
   5.
   6.
   7.
   8.
   9.
  10.

A week of so before the exercise select one person from each team you intend to have, eg four teams, four people (they must be fairly strong characters). Brief them in private, swear them to secrecy and tell them that their job is to get the Holy Bible as high up the list as they can – preferably to number 1. You must be confident that they will keep it quiet; if it leaks, the whole plan will be ruined.

Select your teams carefully. Put known rivals together. If you have people with potential, distribute them among your teams. Put one of your 'briefed' people in each team.

On the day:

- Ask if anyone has ever come across the exercise. If they have, ask them to keep it to themselves.
- Before they split into groups, hand out the exercise and allow them five minutes to select their own eight items and then five minutes to arrange them into order, then split into teams.
- Observe what is going on in each team – they should be far enough away from the other team that no one catches on!
- Regroup and get the teams to read out their lists in turn – and explain the object of the exercise!

The exercise certainly produces fireworks – each team cannot understand why one of their members is so absorbed with the Bible! The nearest to the top I've ever seen was second. The girl, an experienced canvasser, was successful because she didn't push for first; her team, who tried to recognise her reasoning and wanted to pacify her, offered her second! Those who *pushed* for first went over the top and the team ended up totally ignoring them. The moral is – don't push, persuade!

Charades

Role playing is useful both individually or in a group. First set the scene by explaining that one person will be the telesales person, another the prospect and another will analyse the call. Once you name the people to do the charades (you rarely get volunteers for this), ask the other members to make notes for discussion later – you don't want anyone falling asleep! Explain what they will be selling from your own product range, and who the prospect is from the limited information you have; for example, an advertisement in a local paper. You also need to point out that it is obviously more pressurised than in a real-life situation because charades can reduce the most confident of your team to a nervous wreck when they are called upon to perform in front of everyone! Stress that it will help other members as it leads to group discussion and opens avenues of alternative approaches, which is the main aim. You must never pick on weaker members first and must be seen to encourage even the worse blunder with the utmost diplomacy.

Start the charade with a verbal telephone ring after you've established everyone is ready. Once it has begun, make notes as you would with a side-by-side individual training session. If the salesperson becomes stuck don't let her give up – guide her back onto the right track. At the end ask her what she thought of it first and how she feels – usually terrible but relieved it's over. Next ask for the assessor's comments followed by the team's and finally your own observations, remembering to praise, criticise, praise.

Often in a charade situation, even the most experienced of telesales people, when playing the part of the prospect, will be extremely kind. They almost fear to object because it may be their turn to be the telesales person next! If this happens, write out a series of objections on individual cards and at the beginning of a charade session ask the prospect to pick a card 'out of the hat'. She will then be obliged to use the objection stated but without the pressure of being labelled the bad guy! It also ensures that all the likely objections will eventually be covered in the training session.

Another way of using charades is to get everyone to participate on the sales side. These are called 'grasshopper' charades. With this type of charade you are the prospect and you select at random, throughout the sale, different team members to follow through the charade. You will appoint one person to start the sale, and when you want to move on, just tell another person to take over. This keeps everyone on their toes and can be great fun. There should be natural pauses for you to swap people during the sale – usually at each stage in the AIDA sequence – but you can interrupt and swap at any time.

Who am I?

This is a form of quiz but it allows individuals to participate without pressure. Before the session prepare one of the salespeople – in absolute secrecy – to research a famous person, for example a pop star or member of the Royal Family. At the beginning of the session tell the others that they are going to need to use all their questioning techniques to draw information from the appointed member to discuss her identity. Certain questions – for example, 'What is your name?' – will not be answered. To make it harder you can insist that the only answers they will receive are 'yes', 'no', 'irrelevant' or 'no comment'. This will help your staff to think 'on their feet' – not unlike an actual call.

There are all sorts of ways in which you can make your training sessions more interesting and light-hearted. You could integrate these types of sessions with more formal ones by planning ahead; for example:

- **Week 1** Preparation
- **Week 2** Revision openings
- **Week 3** Establishing the need
- **Week 4** Who am I?
- **Week 5** Presentation
- **Week 6** Closes
- **Week 7** Quiz
- **Week 8** Objections
- **Week 9** Film
- **Week 10** Charades

To pitch the more formal sessions at the right level you will have established individual training needs and requirements, remembering, for example, that a new recruit should not be asked to demonstrate their knowledge in a way that makes them feel isolated. Draw on individuals. Ask them to give examples of their experiences – how they handled an objection or what they found difficult during the week. Encourage group participation as this in turn promotes team spirit.

Training material and aids

Anyone speaking to a group of people hopes for a receptive audience. In training this is vital. You want your staff to learn but in order to do this they must want to participate. This can be achieved by making full use of audio-visual aids. We know from people's learning patterns that more knowledge is retained if, first, they are receptive, and secondly, more of their senses have been exposed – especially by means of visual and audio. To stimulate these senses there are a variety of props we should make full use of in training. By doing this we are helping to stimulate the individual's receptiveness and ultimately her retention of the knowledge. Even the most ardent student can only concentrate on oral teaching for a maximum of 40 minutes. As we want to inspire our staff, not deflate or bore them, we should use as much of the apparatus available to us as possible.

There are a number of important features in learning and it is useful to know that:

- we speak at about 120 words per minute;
- we read at about 200 words per minute;
- we listen at about 400 words per minute.

Don't waste the differential – the listener's mind is only partly engaged. Supplement the oral input with visual displays to stimulate thinking activities.

Flipchart or blackboard

Ensure the board is clean and that you have a variety of coloured pens and chalk. Check that your writing is legible and large enough to be seen from the back of the room. You can prepare sections of the session in advance for reference and also write down points as they are brought out in the session. Make sure that when you use the board during the session you don't 'hog' it or speak to it. Establish the point facing your staff then withdraw to the board and chart it. Once you have done this, move to the side so that everyone can see and make any relevant comments. You can then allow your staff to absorb the message visually and make any notes they may wish (always encourage note-taking).

This type of apparatus can also boost a trainee's confidence and ego as they can see their contribution clearly charted and receiving the recognition it deserves.

Overhead projector (OHP)

This piece of equipment can be an asset or an absolute disruption depending on how skilfully it is used. First ensure you have the right materials – acetate pens and paper. Next prepare the acetate, making full use of the sheets within the parameters of the screen. Use capitals for headings and upper and lower case for the body copy. Illustrations and diagrams are also useful and can be extremely eye-catching. Some firms type information onto the sheets – this is largely useful for showing forms, etc but a waste of time and effort for sales training sessions as the text looks boring and usually makes you squint or strain your eyes to see it.

Once you have completed your acetates, mount them on the appropriate borders of card and separate them with plain white paper to keep them clean and tidy. Your OHP should then be positioned securely on a table in an unobtrusive spot. Ensure the apparatus is working correctly and reflecting onto a blank wall or screen. Next adjust the focus and check that all the acetates show up clearly. Sort the acetates into sequence before starting the session – there is nothing worse than watching someone fumble through the sheets. In presenting the session there are certain guidelines to follow:

1. Switch the OHP on *after* you've placed the acetate down correctly.
2. Maintain eye contact with your staff and only glance to the screen occasionally.
3. If you need to refer to individual points use a pencil, not your hand (which will reflect tenfold on the screen) and keep your eyes on the acetate, not the screen. By doing so you will still be facing your audience.
4. If you have several points on one acetate but want to refer to only one at a time, use a piece of card to cover the other points then slide the card down to reveal each other point as necessary.
5. When you wish to change the acetate or talk about something else, switch the OHP off or it will distract your staff.

The correct use of an OHP is essential. It should be seen to enhance your session, *not* distract from it, so use the guidelines and practise using the apparatus until you feel comfortable.

Projector/video machine/carousel

You can either buy or hire equipment and films. Of the three a video machine will be the most useful for training sessions although carousels can be used in making presentations to people about the company or products and are more easily transported. There are a number of national firms that sell or hire out training films and videos. While they can be quite expensive to buy they can usually be hired quite reasonably – the size of your company and your own needs will determine your choice. There are a great many telesales training films available and choosing the right ones can be difficult. Video Arts, who are based in Central London, are well worth contacting for appropriate guidance. They are renowned for using humour to help make the training message stick. Indeed, John Cleese, one of the co-founders, features in a number of them. Other professional and recognised actors demonstrate how, and how not, to tackle certain aspects of sales, which helps staff to relate to their own work. They are certainly well worth looking into.

Manuals/handouts

Each member of staff should have her own training manual in which she can keep her own notes and any handouts to refer to as she wishes. Over the year a great deal of information can be amassed and it is extremely important for telesales personnel to have this information for reference. The number of handouts you issue will largely depend on the topic but should include company policy, product, sales technique, marketing information, etc and the trainee's own notes. Check the manuals from time to time to make sure they are up to date and that the presentation is orderly.

Examples of training sessions

1. Preparing the call

Materials:

- OHP;
- acetate illustrating traffic lights using red, amber and green for the lights;
- flipchart/blackboard and pens;
- cue cards with prompters and objective.

Introduce the session by asking staff to think about their holidays, where they are going and what they need to take. Using a spider chart put *holiday* in the centre. Ask for examples of what they would need to take – passports, suncream, foreign currency, camera, insect repellent, clothing, etc should be forthcoming. Chart these down as the spider's legs as shown in Figure 9.2 (page 92).

Next summarise the findings and get everyone to acknowledge that there is a great deal to think of. This leads to the point of your session – that preparation is very important in anything, especially in your work. Then ask *why* it is important. The answer should be success, job satisfaction, client approval, bonus, etc. Then state the objective of the session:

> At the end of this session you will be able to answer questions on, and write down, what preparation is essential to any call and be able to demonstrate this practically when using the phone.

Next, using a clean board generate another spider chart focusing on *Preparation of a call*. Ask what is needed and why. The answers are opening questions, relevant questions, testimonials, idea of prices and orders, anticipating objections, etc. You will need to guide the answers by posing the questions skilfully; for example;

Question: How are you going to establish two-way communication?

Answer: Ask an opening question.

Question: What will the prospect need to know about our products?

Answer: Benefits, etc.

As answers are given, chart them down and expand on them.

Next use the OHP traffic lights acetate, cover it with card and switch the machine on. Slide the card down to reveal the red light and state that the simple procedure of traffic lights can be implemented in your sales pattern. As you discuss each point, slide the card down to reveal the next stage:

- **Stop (red)** – think about what you are going to say to Mr Prospect – are you prepared?
- **Plan (amber)** – get ready – have you prepared opening questions, etc as per the chart?

● **Go (green)** – now you can go ahead and call Mr Prospect.

Ask if there are any questions and answer them. If not, cover the chart, turn the OHP off and recap on the session, asking questions constantly.

Next, assess the success of the session by giving the staff a real-life example, eg a newspaper cutting of the prospect, and ask them to prepare the call. Check the results, then go back to the objective.

Finally, close the session by asking them to actually go to their desks and contact those leads and monitor the results for the following session. Tell them to remember: 'Nobody plans to fail; they just fail to plan.' Your cue card should look something like Figure 10.2.

Preparation of a call

Introduction
Holiday abroad: Spider preparation F/C
Question: Relate to calls and ask questions
Question: Benefits?
Objective
F/C: Preparation of a call
OHP: Traffic lights – Stop; Plan; Go
Recap
Exercise
Conclusion

Figure 10.2   Example cue card

2. Servicing regulars/increasing territories

All the AIDA aspects should be covered, taking each aspect separately. In addition to looking at ways of bringing in new business, you should also be maximising on existing accounts.

Stress to your staff that in order to increase individual territories, and the overall sales volume, they should not forget the 'bread and butter' money provided by regular clients. Are they just asking for repeat orders or are they looking at each regular individually? Are they informing them of the full extent of the range; showing them how much they value them and generally serving them?

The session should be prepared in the usual way and could follow these lines:

Introduction: In this country we are in the fortunate position of having a full National Health Service. Imagine you were to visit a dentist. What kind of service does he offer? *(Chart the answers on the board – they should include check-ups, fillings, crowning, tooth capping, dentures, dental hygiene, advice and treatment, tooth extraction, etc)* You may have needed a filling on your last visit. On your next visit, however, you wouldn't expect your dentist to just check that one tooth, would you? In just the same way your clients, just because they regularly order the same lines and quantities, it doesn't mean that they are exempt from the full extent of our product range. Do they know what's available to them? Do we have enough information on each to help us help them?

Question: How many of you made your full bonus last week? What was it missed by?

Aims: We will look at ways of achieving targets by maximising on existing accounts so that by the end of this session you will be fully prepared and able to service *all* your accounts effectively while satisfying your customers.

Question: Give me ideas on how we can service our regulars. (Use a spider chart, centre *servicing regulars,* and chart the answers as spider's legs.)

Answer: Ask questions – explore past problems and future worries. Disclose and discuss the full extent of the product range. Understand his business – it's the most important thing to him. Offer testimonials. Suggest specific parts of the range to try, with reasons. Find out if other departments could benefit from your service. Offer contracts, etc. Once you have done this, review your findings.

Exercise: Think about one regular each whom you have neglected and not properly serviced. That one could increase your territory and his turnover. Now start planning, by using the information we've discussed, your approach to him. (Allow 5–10 minutes before making a random selection of staff to tell the group what they propose to do.)

Conclusion: Now that each girl has a plan and specific client in mind, ask them to put it into practice and record the results, which will be reviewed in the next session (at which time you can refer to the aim of the session and assess its success).

Your cue card should look something like the sample displayed in Figure 10.3.

Whatever your session, try to attain as much team participation as is practicable, and vary your use of AIDA to enhance your message.

Servicing regulars

Question:	Dentist – chart service offered – doesn't concentrate on one aspect only.
Question:	Bonus achievement?
Aim:	
Question:	Spider chart – servicing regulars – review
Exercise:	5–10 mins then discuss
Conclusion:	Put into practice – record – review next week

Figure 10.3 Example cue card

3. Closing the sale

Introduction: After you have presented the product using selling points and benefits, cushioning the cost and offering success stories in support of reasons to buy, your prospect still may decline to make an order. The onus is on you to induce a sale.

Question: How can you do this?

Answer: Close the sale.

Aim: Closing the sale means skilfully tying up the loose ends, confirming that the prospect is in favour of purchase and making that buying commitment. It is as crucial to the sale as water to fish! In order to close the sale successfully we need to be aware of certain factors in addition to knowing what types of close are available. By

	the end of this session you will know when to close and which type to use.
Question:	When should you try to close the sale?
Answer:	As early as possible in the sale.
Question:	You should always be looking for an indication of a prospect's interest. This can be helped with the use of tie-downs. What is a tie-down?
Answer:	A buying signal.
Question:	These usually come in the form of questions: 'How much will it cost?'; 'When do you deliver in our area?', etc. If he was completely uninterested he wouldn't waste his time asking you questions. Look out for buying signals and close in on them when appropriate. Remember though that a series of buying signals alone will not produce a sale. A salesperson who echoes the AIDA pattern through to the close, only to omit it, fails. Leaving the end open is disallowing any real commitment to purchase. Another equally important factor is knowing how to pose the closing question/statement. Saying, 'Do you want to buy this, Mr...?' leaves you wide open to a 'No' response – and it does happen. So we need to tailor specific closes to specific situations. What types of close are available? (At this stage run through examples of closes, ie alternative choice, assuming acceptance, boomerang.)
Question:	Once you've asked the closing question what should you do?
Answer:	Remain silent.
Conclusion:	There is a saying in selling – *He who speaks first loses!* The silence provokes a certain amount of pressure on *both* parties to speak. Keep the pressure on the prospect to respond. When he does, it will be either to agree and place an order or to disagree, in which case he will object. If he does, you can then overcome the problem and start again. (Practise the closes in given situations and finally recap by going back to the aim and asking spot questions before concluding.)

4. Handling objections

The final session is probably the most crucial training session you will have to deal with. To master the handling of objections requires skill and confidence. Once staff can deal with them it automatically boosts their confidence as their proficiency and success rate increase. Chapter 6 covers objections in some detail. Use it well and tailor it to your specific needs.

Introduction:	How often do you present our products to a prospect using the AIDA pattern without any prospect interruptions? How often will they immediately say, 'Yes, I'll buy your product'?
Answer:	Hardly ever. (This will probably provoke a few nervous giggles!)
Question:	Objections are as natural to the sale as the presentation and yet you fear them. Why? (A golden opportunity to allow staff to let off steam and show their fears and anxieties.)
Question:	Let us look then at why people object. Is it because they are naturally awkward?
Answer:	No.
Aim:	On the whole it's because they need more information or have misunderstood what we have said. Remember, only up to 85 per cent of what is said over the telephone is taken in. Our potential clients, bearing in mind what they will have missed, will very likely require more information if they are interested. Often, this interest shows itself in the form of an objection – although the more skilful you are at the presentation stage the less likely it will be that you will encounter many objections. Once they occur though, we need to know how to handle them. By the end of this session you will be more aware of the reasons behind objections and of the way in which they can be skilfully handled. This will increase your competence in sales as seen in the results of future calls made.

Next, as in Chapter 6 look at the types of objection that occur most frequently within your organisation. Ask your staff to call them out and chart them on the board. Remember, the more easily and willingly a salesperson handles an objection, the more successful she will be. To an experienced salesperson, a sale without objections is no challenge and therefore dull. A sale can be extremely satisfying and rewarding if an objection is handled successfully.

Next ask staff to look at what they are handling – is the objection 'real' or a 'red herring'? Look at ways of isolating the true objection by using the techniques in Chapter 6.

Organise a charade. Select staff to carry it out and set the scene (which you will already have prepared). Ask the people in the room to think about it for a few moments, then ask them to anticipate the likely objections in the example – chart the answers. Next, give the person chosen to be the prospect a card on which you will have written specific objections – she will be obliged to use them in the charade (you will have ensured that all the tricky aspects are covered). After the charade, discuss it thoroughly and see if the objections raised mirrored those in the charade (they should have done). You could then look at a few more examples before summarising and concluding the session.

For the two latter sessions examples draw up cue cards along the lines of those shown in Figures 10.2 and 10.3.

Setting targets and motivating staff to achieve

A trainer needs to be seen as a leader. By using leadership qualities effectively the trainer can create in staff the will and ability to 'do' through motivation.

As targets need to be achieved to keep companies in profit, techniques need to be applied when giving targets to individuals. First, let's look at the options available in setting targets.

1. **Percentage bonus:** Decide what the overall needs of the company are in terms of sales. How much money do you need to break even? Over and above that figure, how much are you prepared to pay staff for putting you into the realms of profit? If the average breakeven point is, say, 20 sales then you may wish

to pay 5 per cent on 21–25 sales, 10 per cent on 26–30 and so on. Alternatively, you could pay a rounded 2 per cent bonus on everything sold.

2. **Target on money:** For every £1,000 sold the staff would receive, say, 2 per cent.

3. **Set targets:** A fixed bonus could be allocated for specific areas, for example £5 for the first £2,000, £10 for £3,800 and so on. The higher the achievement level, the greater the reward increase should be.

4. **Team targets:** In addition you could have a target to encourage people to help each other; for example, if the whole team achieves X then they will receive YZ. All targets must show clearly what is required, for what period, and what the rewards are.

One school of thought believes that bonuses should be paid on all telephone sales while others believe that they should only be made after a required level of sales has been achieved. This is debatable but the latter makes more business sense. As staff are employed as salaried salespeople then their job is to sell – but how much? Targets can act as an incentive. You don't want to encourage staff to just sit back and relax on Wednesday afternoon if they've achieved their top target. There should be an element of 'the more you sell the greater your earnings'.

The types of target you choose and the financial arrangements are largely personal and individual. They should show individuals that the company does recognise effort and results by offering a comprehensive bonus structure. It is accepted that people appreciate recognition. Occasionally targets may seem abnormally high but many factors attribute to this, eg what was achieved last year, rising costs in rent, production, etc. The trainer needs to go through targets with staff individually – showing why they were set, how they can be achieved, and so on. The trainer will be successful if the staff are – the whole company will benefit and this needs to be stressed. A trainer can help staff achieve their targets by explaining them, looking at areas of the sales they can improve upon, researching new avenues for leads, etc. The salesperson should see that the assistance will ultimately help her to receive not only financial rewards but recognition by her supervisor and manager.

Team meetings on targets and keeping people up to date on

company performance will help to make staff feel part of the organisation, recognise their worth and help them strive to achieve.

Monitoring success

Keeping track of an individual's successes and failures can be aided by keeping records of projects and training and referring to the administrative systems you have introduced. While individual and team coaching enlightens you to immediate problems it may not present an overall picture of an individual's needs. Systems such as daily record forms obviously help the staff to keep track of customers on a daily basis but can also help a trainer, as a pattern may emerge that isn't obvious when you sit with someone for an hour. For example, you may see that a large number of calls show no contact with the decision maker – perhaps the salesperson isn't checking when Mr Prospect is likely to be in, or making a note of the time. A simple mistake but a costly one, both to the company and to the salesperson in terms of bonus. You may also identify that many of the reasons for 'no sale' are because the product is too expensive – the salesperson obviously needs training on handling cost objections.

Each client should have a record card. This too can show a pattern. Perhaps Mr X is regularly placing the same order because the salesperson hasn't offered him the new range, or tried to increase the order. Use the system to your advantage.

Likewise you will need to keep your own records of an individual's projects and training to ensure you haven't missed relaying anything vital or that a salesperson hasn't been absent every time you've shown a certain film, etc. To do this you need two sheets/record cards for each member of staff – one for 'on' job training and one for 'off' job training. You will need a series of headings for each sheet as shown in Figure 10.4.

The signature on the record card is important for 'on' job training. Review the session and ask the salesperson to sign if she agrees with it, eg she now knows how to overcome a cost objection. If she doesn't agree then she needs more training. Next time you sit with her you can recap on the last session and point out that you will be watching out for her presentation of the cost using the techniques learned and that she had difficulty on closes. The new session could be on that, and so on.

Name of trainee:				
Task covered	*Duration*	*Comments*	*Signature*	*Date*

Figure 10.4   Training record sheet

To run an efficient and happy telesales unit you need to keep tight control of what is going on. By enabling yourself, through using the systems I've mentioned, to monitor individuals, you will be helping staff to achieve their targets professionally. From this your team will become more motivated through their own performance, which in turn leads to a higher input, at a more professional level, from each trainee.

Staff appraisal

Targets need to be achieved to improve company performance; but to succeed, staff need to be aware of the importance of improving their own abilities. Encourage self-analysis – by guiding staff to do this you will help them to achieve their targets through isolating their own weaknesses. Group discussion aids self-analysis while inviting others' opinions and allows information and expertise to be pooled under your guidance. Qualities for success lie not only in product knowledge and selling skills but, more importantly, in belief in the job. By training you help elevate confidence, which instils enthusiasm, resulting in improved performance. Self-analysis cannot be reached until a full understanding of the role has been developed. Once this has been achieved then it should walk hand in hand with continual training. When you come to appraise your staff and give them the recognition they have earned, you will look at all aspects of their role on paper. By devising a tick chart you can encourage staff to be critical of themselves (see Figure 10.5).

They need to know how, and on what, they are being measured. Ask them to be as honest and as accurate as possible. Decide on a grading system and then, if they have been properly trained, their answers should tally with mirror your own assessment.

When you come to give appraisals make it a formal event. Staff must realise the importance of assessment at all times; appraisal, which should include an overall grade as shown in Figure 10.5, should echo this.

The five Ws

In order to appraise someone you need to establish the facts. You can't say it is 'good' or 'bad' to arrive at your destination in 40 minutes without making a comparison – it is good or bad in relation to what? What you can say is 'You were late five times' if the facts are in front of you. The five Ws will help in your preparation of appraisals:

What are you measuring?

What were the targets and what was achieved? Facts about selling ability, timekeeping, administration, sickness record and reliability will need to be covered as well as assessing a person's attitude through your observation. If a top target was £1,000 per week and your telesales person achieved 99 per cent, she has failed in her objective. However, as far as departmental standards go she may be the top salesperson, making her the leader – that is a subjective measure. There are, then, two sides to an appraisal – the *objective,* which is the fact of the target, and the *subjective,* which is the method of measuring compared with departmental standards. An appraisal is a critical part of a person's development: 'Ninety per cent of your performance is good, Mary, but I want to talk to you about the extra 10 per cent that is not so good.'

Why do you appraise?

You carry out an appraisal to evaluate performance and obtain results. It also helps you to identify training needs and subsequently develop people in their job. A person's success will act as a great motivator and incentive to improve.

Assessment form

Name:
Date:
Period covered:

| **Product knowledge** | *Grade* | *Comments* |
Your company and products
Competitor's company and products
Client's company and products

Administration
Tidiness
Record cards (client)
Daily record sheets
Diary – use of
   queries – how handled
Accuracy

Call
Voice
Preparation and planning
Aim of call (objectives)
Opening the sale
Questioning techniques
Establishing the need
Listening skills
Presenting benefits
Objections
Closes

Attitude
Enthusiasm
Positivity/optimism
Tact
Initiative
Empathy
General behaviour
Keeping appointments
Customer relations

Overall grade:
Comments:

Figure 10.5   Assessment form

When should you appraise?

You should constantly be appraising – appraisals should be part of an ongoing process informally; then once every 6–12 months you can conduct the formal written/verbal version.

Who should be appraised?

Everyone in the company should be appraised, from the managing director down. Staff should realise that no one is an exception to the rule.

Where do you carry out appraisals?

Appraisals should take place in private – this is an absolute must. The session should be constructive, formal and free from any interruptions.

Structure of the appraisal interview

An appraisal is very like a job interview where you and the person being appraised will each listen, talk and ask questions.

- At the start of the appraisal interview put your telesales person at ease and help her to relax by asking her about, for instance, a recent achievement – something she'll want to talk about.
- Next examine her job description and explain the format of the appraisal. Run through the assessment form headings and the sections it covers. Explain how she has been assessed, ie target achievements, attitude, etc. Then run through the grading system, for instance A = outstanding achievement, B = very good, C = average/acceptable, D = below average, E = unacceptable.
- Discuss performance and look at the individual's lack of knowledge or skill at the job in terms of length of service and expected performance. Give advice on future development.
- Use open-ended questions to lead the individual to discuss and analyse how personal improvements can be made.
- Decide on a plan of action to be agreed together – nothing you have gone through at the appraisal should come as a surprise to her and she should already be aware of her weaknesses.
- Finally, give an overall grade – compare it with the last appraisal if applicable. If a C was awarded on the last two occasions, for

instance, it doesn't mean she hasn't improved – now she has more experience the standard has been raised to take that into account. Maintaining a grade shows that she has been able to keep up with the required performance for her own experience and length of service.

- Conclude by summarising all the main points and agreeing a follow-up procedure. Invite the telesales person to ask questions throughout – this is a golden opportunity for her to air her views and constructively help you in your management of that individual. The success of the appraisal interview is your responsibility and should be handled skilfully and objectively. Encourage her to talk about her career progression, if applicable, but be realistic.
- Finally, give a copy of the appraisal, marked 'strictly confidential', to the individual, and close the interview.

Improving performance needs regular monitoring. By understanding and developing your staff's skills you are helping them to win more business, which ultimately enables your company to achieve its goals, making it more profitable and in a position to expand. Achieving targets also allows your staff to benefit from the financial rewards of bonus; they will find security and job satisfaction.

Finally, encourage staff to keep reviewing their performance, as you no doubt will, and strive to improve day by day regardless of their achievements yesterday.

In addition to in-house training, your call centre or company may consider external training for you and your staff. Indeed, university awards can be gleaned in areas such as 'team leadership' through direct and open learning. If this is a route you'd like to take, contact a company like MDP (Management Development Partnership) on 01248 671617 or any local university.

Ten basic rules of appraisal

1. There should be no surprises – appraisals should be part of an ongoing process.
2. Be honest and frank with your staff. Appraisals without absolute honesty serve no purpose.
3. Appraisals are concerned primarily with performance but not solely with objectively measured performance so you must work closely with whoever is being appraised.
4. A well-structured appraisal system enables staff to recognise ability and is indicative of promotional material.
5. Appraisals should not be subject to a 'halo' or 'black mark' effect – the overall impression needs to be constructive and positive.
6. By nature, appraisals are critical analysis, and can therefore have a negative effect. Eradicate this during an appraisal interview by stating the procedure and purpose at the beginning.
7. Allow for nerves – this is the major 'face-to-face' confrontation with the boss; make the telesales person feel at ease.
8. Stress its importance and the reasons for its formality.
9. Go through the whole appraisal form – if necessary reading the objectives twice and then the results.
10. Look for areas that are not good – put the salesperson's performance under a microscope, turning her weaknesses, through training, into strengths.

11

Get it 'write'! How to formulate successful scripts and letters

We have already looked briefly at information pointers or sales scripts to aid the telesales performance and correct use of AIDA. This chapter now looks at how to formulate good scripts in different situations and sales letters. They all follow the same pattern of a sale and can be adapted to suit your own requirements.

Cold canvassing scripts

When you are canvassing new prospects, invariably you will need to find out who the decision maker is, so all scripts should start with:

> 'Good morning/afternoon, could I have the name of the person who handles XY? or 'Who runs the AB department?', etc.
> 'May I speak to him, please?'
> 'Good morning/afternoon, Mr... My name is... from... I wonder if you could give me some information, please?'

Once you have identified yourself and used your prospect's name, the script should outline the AIDA pattern and give variety and alternatives for staff to use.

Product 1: Careers convention to be held in a major town centre in autumn

Prospect: Personnel managers/training officers

Aim: To sell stands at the event to companies that employ staff.

Opening questions: What percentage of staff start straight from school/college and what percentage come from other companies?

What types of jobs are available for school leavers?

In your opinion would graduates be better prepared to make crucial career decisions when starting full-time work if they spent 12 months in employment before going to college/university?

Interest: When you are recruiting, what percentage of applicants would you say are totally unsuitable for the jobs advertised?

Why do you think that is?

Which types of vacancy are the most difficult to fill?

How important to you is getting the right kind of staff?

Need/committal: If people had a better understanding about your company and its needs it would help you in future recruitment, wouldn't it? *or*

If the time spent on recruitment was condensed it would free you to concentrate on other equally pressing functions, wouldn't it? Well, that's exactly why I'm ringing.

Presentation: List selling points and benefits; for example:

Forward planning – more organised

Helping community – good PR

Your company – experience and reputation

Event and venue – central and convenient

Dates – after holidays and people preparing for final year of education

Publicity – extensive, therefore more response

Refreshments – convenience

Testimonial:	Of previous event if applicable
Cost:	£XY and stand arrangements
Close:	Would you prefer a centre stand or a corner position?
	Will you require any extras for your stand or will the basic provisions be sufficient?
	Would you prefer to be near the entrance or on the back wall?

Product 2: Machine replacement parts

Prospect:	Manufacturing companies – company buyer/owner/manager
Aim:	To sell parts to companies for storage and emergencies
Opening questions:	I noticed your advertisement in *XY* magazine; tell me, are you a regional or national company? (If national it may be a head decision.)
	What types of customer do you have and where do they come from?
Interest:	What type of machinery do you use?
	What is its life expectancy?
	To what extent do breakdowns have an effect on production?
	So it's costly, isn't it?
	Obviously machinery can need a variety of replacement parts at any time, isn't that right?
Need/Committal:	Because of deadlines it must be important to you that you are able to attain quality parts from a reliable source, isn't that right?
	That's exactly why I'm ringing.
Presentation:	Company reputation – reliable
	Products – variety and large stocks, comforting
	Expertise/success – testimonials
	Brand names – established/recognised
	Delivery immediate – no delays
	Delivery cost calculated on order size – save money
	After-sales service – security
	Guarantee – reliability

After-hours phones – to cope with emergencies 24 hours a day

Vast stock – competitive prices

Cost: £X with free delivery within 15 miles

Close: When would you prefer delivery of stock X or Y?

Which part of our range would you prefer to try first, A or B?

Product 3: Estate agency and services

Prospect: Private home sellers advertising in local press

Aim: To make appointments for valuers to call

Opening questions: I noticed you were advertising your house in the *XY Star*; tell me, what kind of response had you anticipated?

How in the past have you sold your properties?

Interest: Why have you decided to sell the house privately?

How much of your time does it take?

Are you asking enough for your property?

Need/Committal: So it's quite time-consuming and possibly risky, isn't it?

That's exactly why I'm ringing.

Presentation: Company reputation, etc – credible

Free valuation and no obligation – nothing to lose but everything to gain!

No sale no charge – only pay when you sell and we're confident you will

Testimonial – success rate

Sales board and photographs free – value for money

Surveyors – accurate valuation so you don't undersell yourself

Computer mail list – select your prospects and mail information to them

Viewing – by appointment or with agent – convenient

Cost: One and a half per cent plus advertising and VAT

Close:	When would it be convenient for our surveyor to call, morning or afternoon? Would you like a signboard or do you prefer to keep the sale anonymous?

Product 4: Annual holiday magazine

Prospect:	All holiday traders
Aim:	To sell annual publication to a large variety of holiday traders and ultimately makers
Opening questions:	When, in the post, has been your most popular period? How much would it cost to stay...?
Interest:	From what area, in the past, have you found most of your custom has come from? What kind of people are you trying to attract?
Need/Committal:	So as I see it, what you are looking for is... isn't that right? That's exactly why I'm ringing.
Presentation:	Product – reputation of being safe, tried and tested and reliable Circulation – saturating your marketplace Type of readers – percentage applicable January publication – people start thinking about holidays Annual publication – referred to all year therefore cost-effective
Cost:	£X = £Y per month for a projected return of £Z
Close:	Would you prefer a bold border or a simple line? Would you like to use artwork or straight text?

Regular canvassing scripts

To service a regular customer the AIDA pattern still needs to be followed. Are you maximising on your orders? Are your clients fully aware of the extent of your range?

Product 1: Coffee machines and associated products

Prospect:	Businesses – all departmental managers
Aim:	To encourage clients to use all your products
Opening questions:	Mr Witt, last time we spoke you expressed your delight with our coffee products.
Interest:	Were you aware that we also supply sugar and dried cream?
	It would be far more convenient to order from one supplier, wouldn't it?
Need:	Extra products – variety
	Reputation – reliability
	Cost – value for money
Cost:	Each container of dried cream will give you X cups at 1p per cup. Your corner shop could cost that and you would be cutting out on shopping time and inconvenience.
Close:	Would you prefer our gold variety or silver?
	Would you like delivery with your coffee or separately?
Additional:	I know you look after the production side; tell me, who manages the accounts side? Would he be the person I would need to speak to about our products in that department?

Always look at ways of maximising on each call. If your client starts decreasing his orders, find out why and either offer an alternative or suggest a solution.

Attach a separate sheet to each sales script, whether cold or regular, covering the likely or actual objections and solutions. Although handling objections should be spontaneous, the additional information will act as an initial refresher.

Sales letters

A sales letter needs to activate a favourable response just as a call does. Some clients will ask you to send information to them after an initial phone contact, so your message must mirror the AIDA conversation

Dear ...	
Attention:	*People need holidays*, and the time is ripe for you to go after all those potential clients who have been hibernating during winter.
Interest:	With the ever-accelerating cost of living and redundancies, people are taking longer than ever to make decisions on their holidays.
Need:	However, surveys show most people still have at least one well-deserved holiday – so why do you still have vacancies?
Presentation:	Advertising in *Holidays GB* could be the solution. It works so successfully that people come back to us year after year. It reaches your best prospects economically – the people who have a 'want' – and turn to our publications to fill it. *Holidays GB* have been running their highly successful publication for ten years now and it enables you to captivate an audience of over 3 million readers each year. Can you afford *not* to join our already successful business people who use it?
Close:	The readers are interested, our clients satisfied – and that's the name of the game! For expert help and advice contact Nikki on Aylesbury 0000 and fill those vacancies now!
Yours sincerely	
Nikki Fallon	
Sales Representative	

Figure 11.1   Holiday magazine sales letter

you have had. Prepare letters in advance, so that you can run them off as required. Let's assume you require a letter to follow up Example 4, annual holiday magazine, in cold calling scripts. A potential holiday advertiser has asked you to send details through (see Figure 11.1).

	Penny Express
A	How is it?
I	A man wakes up in the morning after sleeping on an advertised bed in advertised pyjamas. He will bathe in an advertised tub, wash with advertised soap, shave with an advertised razor, have breakfast of advertised cereal and toast, toasted in an advertised toaster, put on advertised clothes, and glance at his advertised watch. He'll ride to work in an advertised car, sit at an advertised desk, and write with an advertised pen.

| D | Yet this man hesitates to advertise, saying that advertising doesn't pay. Finally, when his unadvertised business goes under he'll advertise it for sale in... |
| A | *The Penny Express.*
We'd rather promote your business than sell it!
Tel: 00000 011111 and ask for... now. |

Figure 11.2   Local newspaper sales letter

You can play on words with your sales letters to get the message across. I once saw a letter from a local newspaper which was effectively illustrated with cartoons and read along the lines shown in Figure 11.2.

An estate agent promoting his service with a competition could send a letter like the one in Figure 11.3.

A	How many of you think you're a fair judge of the property market?
I	Here's your chance to prove it. We have put together a special property competition for you. All you have to do is guess the selling price of each house illustrated below. The first correct answer drawn will receive £1,000 cash towards their moving costs.
D	If you are thinking of selling your property we would be delighted to help. We deal in all types of houses, whether old or new, urban or rural, and offer a sophisticated and complete estate agency service. In fact, whether you enter the competition or not you'll win with us. We would be only too happy to discuss your property with you – completely free of charge and without any obligation.
A	It's your move! Don't delay – ring... on... today for more details.

Figure 11.3   Estate agent's sales letter

The letter would then illustrate the competition and provide the full entry rules.

Personalised letters are an extremely popular way of obtaining extra business from existing clients either by promoting special offers or by offering perks in the form of gifts or extra discounts, etc if they introduce you to new customers.

A credit card company, for instance, may offer jewellery for sale encouraging card holders to use their card (Figure 11.4).

Dear Mr Powell

A   A N Other Credit Cards invite you to wear the classic style and elegance of Jems, whose name has been synonymous with excellence in design and craftsmanship for over 20 years.

I   We are proud to offer our card members the opportunity to own a superb Jems necklace specially selected to appeal to those with a taste for life's luxuries.

D   *(The body copy would describe the appearance of the necklace and an illustrative brochure should be enclosed).* Whether for yourself or for that special someone, a Jems necklace will add sophistication to any look – smart or casual, daytime or evening, and at a remarkably affordable price to our card holders.

A   To secure your purchase phone ... on ... today. The offer is only open while stocks last! Order today and experience the luxury of a Jems masterpiece.

Yours sincerely

– – – – – – – – –

Figure 11.4   Credit card company sales letter

Mail order catalogues or fashion shops with their own charge card often invite customers to special events offering wonderful prizes if they introduce a new 'prospect' – see Figure 11.5.

A   **Jonie vouchers worth up to £1,000!**
I   We'd like to invite you to a Jonie Party! Tuesday 9 November is the anniversary of the opening of our branch at Marble Arch.

D   Celebrations start at 6 pm ending around 9 pm and you will have the opportunity to purchase any of our range with a special discount of 10 per cent. Furthermore, if you introduce us to a friend who does not currently hold a Jonie charge card you will automatically be entered into our grand draw offering vouchers worth up to £1,000.

A   Simply fill out the acknowledgement slip and return it to us by Friday 20 October and we will send an invitation for you and your friend for the party.

Yours sincerely

– – – – – – – – –

Figure 11.5   Mail order catalogue advertising an event

The company could then make follow-up calls, after the event, to the named introductions – people who have presumably willingly consented to accepting the invitation!

Mail order is becoming an increasingly popular source of purchase and the response is handled by post and phone (Figure 11.6).

Dear ...	
A	Since you last heard from us there have been plenty of changes for the better at Best Books.
I	For a start, we now *guarantee* that members joining us now will win a prize in the next twelve months if they follow a few simple rules.
D	Second, our catalogues are now sent first class to give you more time to get your entries in before the closing dates of various competitions. Finally, as the annual subscription rate is due to rise at the end of this month it pays to join us now. You'll find a brief reminder in the attached leaflet of how Best Books can help you become a winner. Remember also that variety is the spice of life and that's what we offer our members, with the Best Books choice at special members' prices.
A	All you have to do is pick up the phone and dial... ask for... and your subscription will be renewed. Do it today while you're thinking about it – before the price rises.
Yours sincerely	
– – – – – – – –	

Figure 11.6   Mail order catalogue sales letter

Specialised items need to be sent to a strictly specialist market – preferably named. If, for instance, you are selling courses on interview techniques you will want to attract personnel managers. Registered lists are available for almost any market and while it obviously isn't free it could be worth your while making enquiries. Take a look at Figure 11.7.

Dear Mr Davis	
A	Would you like to reduce your company's time and increase your expertise? Have you thought of buying a word processor?

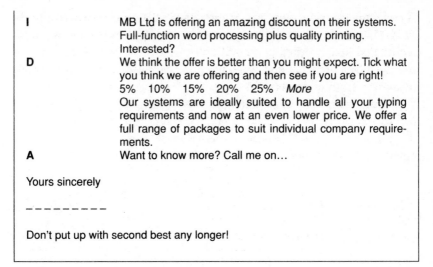

I	MB Ltd is offering an amazing discount on their systems. Full-function word processing plus quality printing. Interested?
D	We think the offer is better than you might expect. Tick what you think we are offering and then see if you are right! 5% 10% 15% 20% 25% *More* Our systems are ideally suited to handle all your typing requirements and now at an even lower price. We offer a full range of packages to suit individual company requirements.
A	Want to know more? Call me on…

Yours sincerely

_ _ _ _ _ _ _ _ _

Don't put up with second best any longer!

Figure 11.7   Specialised sales letter

Dear Sir

A	Would your sales department like online answers to the following questions?
I	1. What is each salesperson actually doing today? 2. Which competitors are most active in your accounts? 3. How often have your top ten customers been visited in the last three months? Of course they would – and now the answers are available.
D	Assured seminars Assured seminars … (You would go on to explain the full extent of your training packages, outlining the reasons for comprehensive training and up-to-date management techniques to keep your managers one step ahead in their work.) *Course Topic Dates Venue* (Listings under appropriate headings.)
A	A member of our marketing team will contact you in the near future to discuss our seminars in more detail. Meanwhile, should you require more information please phone… on… now.

Yours sincerely

_ _ _ _ _ _ _ _ _

Figure 11.8   Sales letter advertising seminars

A company offering seminars could word its letter as shown in Figure 11.8. This letter leaves the door open for the telesales person to recontact the prospect. Whether you follow this system or make calls first followed by letters depends on what you are selling and your back-up resources. Both methods work.

A final word on sales letters – they must be good. Your sales message must be in black and white to be referred to over and over – it's a statement. Make full use of the AIDA pattern. Use testimonials if appropriate, and follow the action through.

12 *Conclusion*

Where do I go from here?

The key to future success lies with you. Remember we live in a world where records and achievements are constantly changing. Mistakes that alienate potential customers can be easily made, but if you are no fool you will survive. The following checklist for self-preservation could help, whether you are in a managerial capacity or on the front line.

- **Remain positive** – your attitude rubs off on others.
- **Keep personal goals high** – striving for perfection helps to keep you challenged and interested. This in turn helps to keep you motivated.
- **Strive to become more knowledgeable** – the more you know, the more you can help your customers. If you are successful in this then your job satisfaction will be greater.
- **Review your performance regularly** – note any changes for better or for worse. It is too easy to become complacent. Keep questioning your own and your staff's performance.
- **Learn from others** – only a fool learns purely from his own experiences. Watch others and listen. Try applying different approaches within the structure of two-way communication.

and finally...

- Aim for continuous improvement – always bear in mind the following: Try to do a little better today that which you did well yesterday.

Index

References in italic indicate figures or tables

Business Enterprise Guides

Published in association with *The Sunday Times*
and the Institute of Directors

The Business Enterprise Handbook: A complete guide to achieving profitable growth for all entrepreneurs and SMEs
Colin Barrow, Robert Brown and Liz Clarke

The Business Plan Workbook, Fourth Edition
Colin Barrow, Paul Barrow and Robert Brown

E-Business for the Small Business: Making a profit from the Internet
John G Fisher

Financial Management for the Small Business, Fifth Edition
Colin Barrow

Forming a Limited Company, Seventh Edition
Patricia Clayton

Law for the Small Business, Tenth Edition
Patricia Clayton

Running a Home-Based Business, Second Edition
Diane Baker

Starting a Successful Business, Fourth Edition
Michael J Morris

Successful Marketing for the Small Business: A practical guide, Fifth edition
Dave Patten

All titles are available from good bookshops. To obtain further information, please contact the publisher at the following address:

Kogan Page Ltd
120 Pentonville Road
London N1 9JN
Tel: 020 7278 0433
Fax: 020 7837 6348
www.kogan-page.co.uk